REVIEWS

"Jennifer Heigl's *Career Diary o[f ...]* handbook detailing the day-to-day responsibilities of the often-challenging-but-always-rewarding real life of a caterer. An essential read for anyone interested in the marketing, cooking, business, management, and financial skills necessary to begin his or her own endeavor."

—Courtney Febbroriello, author of *Wife of the Chef*, owner of Metro Bis Restaurant

"*Career Diary of a Caterer* was easy to read and enjoyable. If you are starting a business in catering, this true account will help you tremendously."

—Mary Lou Burton, owner, Bravo! Publications

"This book is invaluable to anyone wanting to get into the catering business. Just when you think you have read everything you can on catering, here comes an honest look at the industry. Jennifer has really captured the frustration and hard work that can be a part of being a business owner and at the same time, her love and sense of pride and passion for her business really shines through. Anyone interested in starting a catering company should keep a pen and paper with them while reading so that they can take notes on all of the priceless information and tips that Jennifer so graciously passes on. A must have for any culinary school or high school."

—Crystal Reinwald, owner, Subito Catering

"As a newbie, I found this book to be highly insightful. It's a record of what life is really like out here in the food industry. I am thankful to have this book in my tool belt! A "MUST HAVE" for anyone wishing to join us in the pursuit for gorgeous food in a profitable endeavor, all while having a good time."

—TL Anderson, owner, Solchemy

CAREER DIARY™

OF A

CATERER

Thirty days behind the scenes with a professional.

GARDNER'S CAREER DIARIES™

JENNIFER HEIGL

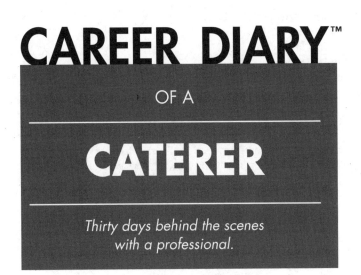

GARTH GARDNER COMPANY

GGC publishing

Washington DC, USA · London, UK

Publisher: Garth Gardner, Ph.D.
Editor: Olive Vassell
Associate Editor: Paul Siegel
Cover Designer: Doh Daiga
Layout Designer: Derek Horton
Concept Designer: Nic Banks
Cover photo: Steve Harmon

Editorial inquiries concerning this book should be mailed to:The
Editor, Garth Gardner Company, 5107 13th Street N.W.,Washington
DC 20011 or emailed to: info@ggcinc.com. www.gogardner.com

ISBN 1-58965-031-X

Library of Congress Cataloging-in-Publication Data

Heigl, Jennifer.
Career diary of a caterer: thirty days behind the scenes with a
professional / Jennifer Heigl.

    p. cm. -- (Gardner's Career Diaries)

ISBN 1-58965-031-X

1. Caterers and catering--United States. 2. Caterers and catering—
Vocational guidance – 3. Caterers—United States—Biography. 4.
Career. I. Title.

TX911.2.H43 2007

642'.4--dc22

                      2007035987

Printed in Canada

TABLE OF CONTENTS

ACKNOWLEDGMENTS

I'd like to thank the following individuals for their assistance on the road to publication. First and foremost, a big thank you to my husband and business partner, Jeff, for sharing his incredible knowledge of the catering and restaurant industry, as well as his continuing love and support of my writing; my daughters, Ella and Sarah, for teaching me that life is short and valuable; my Mom and Jack, for showing me that you have to work hard to be successful – in business, life, and love; my first boss, Neil McCurdy, who always gave me the opportunity to excel; my high school chemistry teacher, Mr. Huber, for teaching me how to problem-solve; my family and friends for their ongoing love; and my marvelous editor, Olive Vassell. Finally, a big thank you to those along my path who have stood in my way, pigeonholed my talents, or believed that I lacked initiative – you only made me work harder.

BIOGRAPHY

Born in northern California in the late 1970s, I moved with my mother and stepfather to southeastern Michigan and grew up in Milan, a small town just south of Ann Arbor noted for its federal prison and local drag races. I was mortified to be trapped in such a place, knowing everyone in town and having them know me. In fact, only recently have I grown to appreciate that sense of community.

My original plans were to become a musician—specifically a singer. My mother, a church choir director, had me performing in front of our congregation by age five. I continued my music studies throughout elementary and junior high by attending music camp, earning a small part in an all-school musical, and singing with local and regional choirs, including one that toured Europe.

I continued to pursue a career in music during high school, but also developed interests in photography, writing and editing. As a high school junior I joined a small vocal ensemble to audition collectively for a regional choir, which we were invited to join. When my choir director learned that I did not have the inclination to compete at the state level, he insisted that I would never succeed in the music business. I took him at his word.

I chose Western Michigan University for its music program, strangely enough, figuring I would be well situated if I ever changed my mind about my career direction. My original major was in public relations, part of the communications curriculum. While studying in Australia during a junior-year-abroad program, I enrolled in one of my first public relations courses and found myself quite dismayed by the course outline. I left the class, chose instead to study graphic design, and never looked back. Returning to Michigan for my senior year, I changed my degree path from public relations to a more general communications studies major, with a minor in graphic arts. My graduation advisor told me he expected to see me back at school in a few years since I "wouldn't be able to get a job with this degree." I told him I'd be back, but only when I was more successful than he was.

Thanks to my skills in graphic design, I was offered a job in 1999, right out of college, as Production Coordinator for a maritime-related dot-com in Seattle, Washington. Within two years I had advanced to the role of Creative Web Producer, working with a team to redesign the company's Web site, maintain our search engine status, and build our brand image through print and online advertisements. It was here that I developed a deep interest in marketing communications, although the dot-com crash led to my layoff, as it did with so many of my colleagues.

In January 2002, my father was changing planes in Seattle and asked if I could drive him and a friend home to Portland rather than wait for their connecting flight. We dined together that evening and his friend, a lovely woman named Janis he'd met on a flight from Portland to Yakima, spoke animatedly about her husband and family. When I mentioned I was having boyfriend troubles, she told me she had a wonderful son near my age who was "in need of a good woman." She spent our three-hour drive that evening describing her son, Jeff, and his culinary and personal accomplishments. Jeff and I met the next day, and we have been together ever since.

I moved to Portland at the end of 2002, where I worked as a marketing assistant with a local company. A year later, Jeff and I decided to combine our talents and start a catering business that featured organic items. Joking that I would marry him if the business went well, we married a year after the business began.

Over the past four years, Zen Kitchen has been recognized for its involvement with non-profit organizations and its donations to the community. We received the "Best Caterer" award by Citysearch.com in both 2006 and 2007, and we have catered events for *Glamour* and *Vegetarian Times* magazines. My role as Director of Marketing is very much a do-everything position, with office responsibilities that include sales and marketing, event management, and looking after our staffing needs. I'm also a regular fixture in the kitchen, where I help with food preparation.

I've truly enjoyed working with Jeff and the rest of our team to promote the consumption of organic foods in the greater Portland area. I also look forward to visiting my college graduation advisor again, real soon.

CURRENT POSITIONS AND RESPONSIBILITIES

My responsibilities tend to vary, depending on the day and what needs to be done. I'm the public face of Zen Kitchen, while Jeff works behind the scenes. He wears the chef's hat, while I have a whole set of them to don.

One of the hats I wear is events coordinator. I spend every morning responding to telephone and electronic inquiries as well as wrapping up loose ends for upcoming events—revising proposals, answering last-minute questions, and confirming orders regarding rental items. I have an assistant who follows up with clients as well but, as one of the owners, I like to oversee and confirm all final details and make sure things are properly organized.

I'm often found at the site of our events—especially those that are large or high profile—where I assist the banquet captain with the room layout, staff assignments and basic time management. In addition to my onsite responsibilities, I coordinate staff assignments and equipment rental for each event, finalize details with the client, participate in a walk-through prior to each affair, coordinate bartending or insurance requirements that may be needed, design the menu cards on display at the buffet table, and provide maps and final billing paperwork for all deliveries.

Whenever I'm not coordinating an event, I like to wear my marketing and Web design hats. These responsibilities include updating photos and text on our company's Web site, managing our search engine rankings and adhering to our marketing plan for the year, plus making contact with new clients and facilitating relationships with existing ones. Jeff and I devise an annual marketing program, broken down into quarterly goals, that includes creating direct-mail materials, attending trade shows, and looking after overall client maintenance. We do a mass mailing at least twice a year, especially after attending a trade show where we acquire a number of client leads. I also contact former clients to see if they're planning anything new and solicit feedback regarding past work. It's important to stay in touch, as word of mouth can be your greatest marketing tool, but it is also vital to be open to client feedback—whether negative or positive. When people know you care about what they think, they are more inclined to hire you again. I coordinate our online banner ads as well as our print advertising. Thankfully, much of our business comes via referral, which keeps our ad budget down.

My favorite hat to wear, however, is as backup preparation (prep) chef. For large events that require an extra set of hands in the kitchen, I enjoy offering my assistance. I love the change of pace when stepping into the kitchen—the adrenaline starts to pump, wonderful smells fill the air, and beautiful food is created. In addition to assisting with the actual food prep, I also help out by coordinating the loading of our delivery van prior to each event. We have a complete list that needs to be checked and double-checked as each vehicle is loaded, including keeping track of food, beverages, serving materials, staff uniforms, and linens. My taking charge of this aspect of the business allows our kitchen staff to continue working on the food, thereby saving us valuable time. In the catering business it's really all-hands-on-deck for every event. You have to be open to doing whatever needs to be done at any given time.

My most boring hat of all involves working in the office. Even though we hire an outside accountant and have an office assistant, I tend to oversee most of the general office duties. These include answering phone calls when needed, picking up the mail, sorting out accounts receivables and payables, working with vendors regarding office equipment and services, following up with clients who have not yet paid their bills, and dealing with whatever sales calls we receive. I also look after the challenging task of hiring and firing workers. Sometimes you have a good day, where everyone shows up with a smile on his or her face. Other times you have a bad one and must let an employee go for being late for the third time. Being a business owner has its perks as well as its down sides—you have to learn to go with the flow. But I wouldn't trade this job for the world!

RESUME

SUMMARY

- More than eight years of experience in advertising, marketing, public relations, event management, copywriting and copyediting in the fields of computer software, retail sales, biotechnology and non-profit organizations.

- More than three years entrepreneurial experience, including all aspects of building a business from the ground up—budget, branding, sales, marketing, and event coordination.

- Extensive knowledge of a wide range of software applications, operating systems and computing languages including Adobe, Microsoft, Macromedia, Windows, Macintosh, FTP and HTML.

- Considerable writing and editing skills in the areas of business and technical writing, plus editorials.

- Articles published in *The Writer magazine*, plus online "'zines" *Nervy Girl* and *Uncapped*.

EMPLOYMENT HISTORY (2003–CURRENT)

Director of Marketing and Events

Zen Kitchen Catering, Portland, Oregon

- Analyzed demographics and determined the

viability of an off-site organic catering business starting up in the Portland (Oregon) metropolitan area.

- Collaborated with the executive chef regarding the company's start-up business plan and its initial budgetary requirements, plus location determination and the acquisition of office, kitchen and event equipment.

- Maintain business office duties including profit-and-loss statements and monthly billings, plus bookkeeping issues such as taxes, payroll and scheduling.

- Manage all external marketing, including direct mail and public relations campaigns.

- Design all advertising and branding items including logo and letterhead, Web site content, search engine placement, and local ads in a variety of printed media.

- Orchestrate off-site events from start to finish, including proposal development, communications to clients, staff scheduling, vendor organization, day-of-event planning, and invoicing.

- Coordinate all in-house communications between seasonal, kitchen and office staffs.

- Manage one in-house marketing person plus off-site service staff.

- Screen all employees prior to hiring.

- Assisted with the development of the Zen Kids

Portland program, an organic school lunch program for K–8 students.

MARKETING ASSISTANT 2002-2003
Columbia Analytical Services, Kelso, Washington

- Designed all marketing materials including information sheets, service proposals, and trade show handouts.

- Composed and maintained internal communications documents as well as Web site content.

- Managed the company's attendance at local and national trade shows, including the coordination of travel arrangements, booth setup, and staffing requirements.

- Organized and maintained trade-show sales leads

- Assisted marketing director with additional marketing and public relations duties.

WEB CARE TECH SUPPORT ADVISOR 2002
The Cobalt Group, Seattle, Washington

- Assisted local and national clients in the use of the company's Web-based CRM software.

- Dealt with customer issues including browser assistance, login and password assistance, plus photo and content maintenance.

- Maintained customer data and troubleshooting steps

via a service tickets database.

- Collaborated with team members and managers to develop more efficient service procedures.

- Promoted departmental goals as a volunteer on the internal departmental communications committee, plus the content migration and customer auditing committees.

- Facilitated the flow of communications among departments, vendors, customers and consultants.

CREATIVE WEB PRODUCER 1999-2001

Yachtworld.com, Seattle, Washington

- Developed numerous branding projects, including the redesign of the company's public identity and the corporate Web site.

- Composed copy for, print ads, banner ads, sales promotions, marketing material, and Web site content.

- Employed Adobe Photoshop and Adobe Illustrator to create and maintain Web site graphics, print ads and banner ads.

- Designed advertising online and in print for placement in a variety of magazines and Web search engine pages.

- Assisted advertising clients with technical issues that included photo retouching and uploading, plus controlled general Web site maintenance for individual broker's pages.

MARKETING COORDINATOR (PART-TIME)
1998–99

Kalamazoo County YMCA, Kalamazoo, Michigan

- Collaborated with the marketing director through all stages of event planning for the annual silent auction fundraiser, including the design and layout of the program booklet, the coordination of advertisers, and facilitating the event's location, food service and entertainment.

- Composed and maintained all internal communications and external promotional material—including calendars, program flyers and enrollment information —for a variety of YMCA programs.

EDUCATION

- B.A. Communications Studies, Western Michigan University, Kalamazoo, Michigan.

- Design & Communications Studies, University of South Australia, Adelaide, Australia.

PREDICTIONS

- *Call in payroll and pay bills*
- *Create proposals and finalize details for various upcoming events*
- *Organize lunch program registrations*

DIARY

The holidays are stressful enough for the general public, but for those of us in the service industry they tend to be even more of a balancing act. It's December 12, and holiday parties are in full swing. November and December tend to be our busiest months of the year, barring the ever-popular wedding season from mid-May to mid-September. Oftentimes we enter November without anything booked and suddenly get bombarded with requests for holiday events, notably around mid-month. While most of the events are office parties, there are a number of private ones as well. People look forward to partying more and cooking less during the holiday season.

Our establishment is located in the southeast part of town, easily accessible to all the major freeways. Most of our catering jobs take place within twenty miles of our kitchen, though we do travel as far as the ocean during the summer for wedding receptions on the beach. This month our events are all in town, ranging in size from 20 to 500 guests, with an average in the 100–150 range.

So far we have seven holiday events booked for December, with inquiries every day from people who want to know which dates are still open. Our office is busy coordinating proposals, scheduling workers, organizing rental equipment, responding to telephone calls and e-mails, and making sure the chef doesn't lose his mind. Today is Wednesday, which means it's payroll day. We employ two full-time staff members, one part-timer, and anywhere from five to fifteen on-call workers. Our payroll numbers have to be in by two o'clock, and I'm already behind.

In the catering business, though, it's always something. You can organize to your heart's content, but something will inevitably come up to disrupt your carefully laid plans. On the first catering job we ever did, we forgot to bring along serving utensils. I panicked and ran downstairs to the building's in-house cafeteria, begging for whatever serving pieces they could spare. Thankfully they helped us out, and the rest of the operation went off without a hitch. The snafus are always somewhat minor, so you learn to think on your feet. No matter if you're catering a plated meal for 300 or a small wedding for 40, you have to learn how to adjust and adapt to any situation.

This weekend's events are somewhat small—none more than fifty guests—but each represents its own challenges. Our host for tomorrow's dinner has come down with a severe cold, and her secretary is busy scrambling to find a new location for the event. We know from past experience that if they're unable to find a location in such a short time, we run the risk of losing the event entirely to a local restaurant or a venue with an in-house caterer. After hunting around most of the morning in an attempt to locate a new venue on such a short notice, the client decides to reschedule for some time in January. While this means one less sale for the week, our chef gives out a sigh of relief and moves his focus to Friday's affair.

It's past lunchtime and timecards have been collected for my regularly scheduled call to our payroll provider. One of our newest jobs involves running a school lunch program for a local private elementary school, so I spend an hour returning phone calls and e-mails from parents who want to sign up their children. Our lunch server arrives from today's meal and begins her chores in the kitchen, which involves rinsing lunch trays, silverware and plastic cups in preparation for tomorrow's meal service. Coincidentally, I also receive a contact through our Web site from another local school interested in our lunch program. I do a little happy dance at my desk. It's exciting for us to bring healthy, organic foods to area schoolchildren.

Our chef, somewhat frantic about this weekend's events, quickly escapes the kitchen duties with a run to the local store for some last-minute items. He is slightly less than thrilled when I pass along the news of the new school, as it will mean more planning and organization for him and his staff. He instructs me to wait for a delivery of wild salmon plus a visit from our local courier who is delivering cases of wine and beer for a literary event next month. Just as I'm signing the courier's paperwork, the phone rings upstairs and I run to my office, barely catching the caller. It's someone trying to sell us something we don't need, so I hang up the phone and ponder what tomorrow may bring.

LESSONS/PROBLEMS

When dealing with multiple events, it's important to stay as organized as possible. Timelines and checklists are both appropriate tools in the catering world, as they help keep staff members in all departments focused on the company's common goals. Each aspect of catering is a team effort, from the office and kitchen organization to event management. We're careful to sit down with departmental leaders each week to determine our goals and tasks for that week. A lack of organization can cause miscommunication, which may result in arguments and consequently carry over into catering an unsuccessful and unprofessional event.

PREDICTIONS

- *Create invoices for upcoming events*
- *Verify delivery information for this week's events*
- *Begin work on upcoming food order*
- *Organize school registrations*

DIARY

I've always disliked Mondays, no matter where I worked. It always seems to take me close to an hour to focus, regroup, reorganize, and get things moving on Mondays.

I show up late today because of a doctor's visit, so the fog hangs around a bit longer. Our lunch assistant has been busy finishing up some assignments for her college classes, so she appears a bit worse for wear having had only a couple of hours of sleep in the past 36 hours. After discussing the situation with Jeff, our chef, we decide to send her home. This means I'll pick up some extra slack in the kitchen, but it's worth it. To quote Delores in the television show, *Dead Like Me*, "A tired worker is a poor worker, and a poor worker is often an out-of-work worker."

Most of our school registrations have arrived, as Friday was the due date. Our numbers appear to be about the same as last semester, which we more or less expected. The number of students served has remained constant over the past two years, although we've increased the number of

JEFF STEPS IN TO SERVE SCHOOL LUNCH WHILE OUR LUNCH MANAGER IS OUT.

lunches we're delivering, which is good. This semester we've changed over to an all-hot-food menu rather than alternating hot with cold. Many parents asked for it, and it's rewarding to note the widespread success our change is having. We made this change after sending out a survey regarding our school lunch program. This element follows one of the most important business rules—listen to your customers. Some parents had an issue with our desserts, so we pulled those from the menu as well. It's important to take into consideration the opinions of your customers. If two people don't like an item, you have to decide if it's important enough to remove it from the menu. It pays to be a smart businessperson, even when catering to ten-year-olds.

Aside from the school registrations, we're also finishing up our holiday events. We have one small drop-off tonight, with a larger event tomorrow evening for a group of local sports executives. There is also a small breakfast drop-off on Friday. After that it's a well-deserved holiday break, and our staff is very much looking forward to it!

For tomorrow's event we need to organize rental items—linens, wine glasses and hors d'oeuvres plates—as well as coordinate with the art gallery where it's being held. Many places like these require additional insurance coverage against damage, should the unforeseen occur. In addition to insurance, locations may have specific rules regarding loading and unloading, rental pickup and delivery, and caterer requirements. This art gallery is a frequent venue for us, so we're both prepared and relaxed.

The kitchen, however, is another story. Busy with the preparation for tonight's small holiday event, our chef is also trying to initialize the prep work for tomorrow's larger party. This usually includes organizing the kitchen equipment, ordering the food, and logging in food items as they arrive. When you're a small organization with limited storage space, it's a challenge to order items in bulk on a weekly basis. Therefore, although we have our monthly bulk order on hand from our national distributor, there are still last-minute trips to be made. Sometimes one local store doesn't have the items our chef needs, which can turn an afternoon into a chaotic scavenger hunt.

We're well into the afternoon, with the kitchen buzzing and

the office winding down. There are a few last-minute phone calls and e-mails to address, and I need to print out driving directions and a final invoice for tonight's drop-off. Tomorrow, everyone will arrive early to organize final details of the art gallery event.

LESSONS/PROBLEMS

Make sure to listen to your customers. Some may provide feedback simply to be heard, but many of them have insights into menu options or event details that you or your staff may have missed. Especially when you have a contractual agreement, such as with our school lunch program, it's important to get regular feedback to keep your clients happy. Maintain an open mind. You never know what you'll learn!

*OUR DESSERT TABLE AT THE ART
GALLERY EVENT.*

Day 3 | *DECEMBER 19*

PREDICTIONS

- *Join the kitchen staff for party preparation*
- *Return phone calls and e-mails*
- *Appear at tonight's event to meet the client*

DIARY

There is always a buzz about the kitchen on the day of a big event. Today we start things a bit late, so our staff members are somewhat frenzied. Due to a power outage in the area, with more than half a million people without electricity, we've been forced to put up with delays on several of our weekly deliveries. Add to that a few staff members out sick, and we're definitely challenged.

Luckily the office is quiet today. With the holidays coming up this weekend, most people have either taken the week off or are not yet booking parties. My assistant and I finalize the details for three events scheduled in January, grab a quick lunch, and then head to the kitchen to assist in food preparation.

The menu tonight is fairly simple, essentially hors d'oeuvres for forty guests and minimal rental requirements. Items include crab-and-parmesan phyllo cups, mushrooms stuffed with Italian sausage, a selection of domestic cheeses, and our specialty dessert item, Zen Bananas. These are chocolate-dipped bananas rolled in toasted coconut. Most of these projects will wrap up quickly, since we only need to prepare around eighty pieces of each item.

By late afternoon the kitchen preparation is complete. We've created almost 500 individual hors d'oeuvres for tonight's event. The kitchen is a mess and there are tons of dirty dishes piled up, but our kitchen staff can breathe a sigh of relief and take some time to eat before the party rush begins in an hour. The supplies are collected from our rental source and our event manager begins the task of checking off the necessary materials to make sure we're prepared. Our checklist includes everything from the menu items to the coats the serving staff will wear, so it's imperative we keep track of what's loaded into the delivery van and what returns to the kitchen after the event. That's how we'll know if anything has gone missing.

It's just a few minutes before we need to leave for our event this evening. The delivery van is packed and our staff has arrived on time. Last-minute preparations include ironing a few wrinkles out of shirts and linens, coordinating the table décor, finalizing the contact and billing details, and assigning an event captain. We have a checklist called the captain's log that gives our event captain an overall view of the event plus details on the client, the menu, and the staff. We always take a final cruise through the kitchen to make sure everything has been packed, and then off we go.

We return to the kitchen at 10:30 P.M. Everything tonight went smoothly. We'd planned for 40 guests but only 25 showed up, which made our jobs even easier. It's always fun to host an event at this gallery, since they change the exhibits regularly. Tonight I was thrilled to see a small Monet display featured in the main room, and I took time to view each piece after setting up the buffet tables. There's something magical about standing alone in the main room of an art gallery. Our parties take place after regular business hours, so the room remains empty except for the art on display. You can stand inches from an original sculpture and take your time to enjoy every curve and bend. At one event, there was a gorgeous bronze statue of a tiger, exquisitely lifelike in design. I glanced at the price tag—only $9000—and warned my coworkers. "No one touch the tiger," I chuckled.

Once our van has been unloaded back at the kitchen, the staff updates their timecards and departs. Some of our younger staff members hit the bars, while those of us who are older generally head home. It's been a ten-hour day and I need the rest. "Don't start a business if you don't like long hours," is yet another warning for budding entrepreneurs. We often put in very long days, especially during certain parts of the year, and many of us wear multiple hats, but there is a certain pride involved after completing an event.

It was nice this evening, for a change, to have fewer guests rather than more. Unfortunately it's a common occurrence in the catering business to have more attendees than the host originally declared. Happily for us, in our four years in business we've run out of food only once. Our kind-hearted chef always has leftovers to donate to the shelter. At his former place of work, a local assisted-living residence, he was tasked with preparing three meals a day for 85 residents, at $3 a day each. For him, having a real budget is a wonderful thing. Being able to donate to local shelters is just the cherry on top.

LESSONS/PROBLEMS

A key lesson in catering is to be ready for anything. After tonight's event there was a fair amount of leftover food. Planning ahead, we made sure to bring along take-home containers and plastic wrap. Many clients, particularly the bigger-budget folks, will often inquire as to the whereabouts of the leftover food items. Our kitchen staff always boxes up the leftover food, complete with labels stating reheating instructions, so our guests can enjoy the food at a later time.

Tonight our guests elected not to take anything with them, so our hors d'oeuvres will be refrigerated and donated to a local homeless shelter in the morning. Food waste should be avoided whenever possible.

DINNER IS PREPARED FOR 300!

Day 4 | *DECEMBER 22*

PREDICTIONS

- *Start the day early, but also finish early*
- *Clean the kitchen and close up shop for the holiday weekend*

DIARY

It's 10:00 A.M. the Friday before Christmas, and I've already been at work for four hours. We catered a small breakfast this morning and, as the owner of a small business, I'm often tasked with working the early shift. After a cup of chai and two glasses of iced tea, I'm surprised I'm not more awake.

Our delivery this morning went well, but breakfast caterings can oftentimes prove difficult. There are moments when

OUR FINISHED PLACE SETTING BEFORE EVERYONE ARRIVED.

Photo: Steve Harmon

you're pleased to be out and about so early—fewer cars on the road, no one else in line at the coffee shop, and scoring the best table in the restaurant for breakfast—but you're still up before the sun. Especially in winter, it's colder, darker and quieter, with more of a temptation to fall asleep at the prep table. On our way to the delivery site today, we ran into early-morning road construction and sat for a while until a slow-moving train cleared an intersection. We arrived at the location a bit late, but our drop-off system is so well ingrained that it only took a couple of minutes to set up the buffet.

With our delivery guy off to retrieve the serving items from this morning's event, our sole kitchen employee begins the winter cleanup prior to closing our offices for the holiday. While many caterers work straight through until New Year's, we try to keep the week after Christmas sacred, allowing everyone time off to be with their families. My office assistant will show up occasionally throughout the week to check telephone messages, but other than that we're off for a much-needed break.

Consequently the day before the holiday break is all about cleaning and organizing. From the grill to sets of dishes, everything in the kitchen is scrubbed clean and dried off. Many items are wrapped in plastic after they're cleaned—chafing dishes, silverware and serving utensils—and placed into hibernation until our first catering job next year. Leftovers languishing in the refrigerator are either revived for donation or carted away in the bins that hold our biodegradable items.

This is also a hectic time for the business side of the operation. We prefer to take care of all payroll loose ends before departing for the holidays, leaving a clean slate for when we return. The end of the year also means closing the books for tax purposes, so my office assistant and I tally up our purchase receipts and event invoices. Sales have continued to double every year we've been in business, so I'm always excited to calculate our final numbers. Everything gets entered into a spreadsheet that goes to our accountant including the equipment we purchased and the advertising we paid for, plus our charitable donations, food orders and countless other details. Finally I pay all remaining bills, ensuring everything's up to date. On the surface it sounds like a madhouse, but after three years of this routine we all operate like a well-oiled machine.

December's events proved quite manageable, a welcome contrast to prior years where much larger holiday events left us almost too tired to enjoy our subsequent time off. During our first year we catered a non-profit function for 350 guests and spent the previous two months planning every aspect of the affair. The night of the event, five staff members worked the hors d'oeuvres reception in one room while seven others hurriedly set up the ballroom for formal dining.

This year we catered the same event at the same location. We were far better prepared this time around, having made the necessary adjustments to accommodate the idiosyncrasies of the service elevators that only traveled between certain floors. Along with adapting our delivery and replenishment schedule from one event room to the other, the transition from stand-up hors d'oeuvres to a sit-down dinner went smoothly. When the mad rush began and everyone poured into the dinner area, our floor captain was prepared with updated notes in her captain's log, including such details as which door would be off-limits to arriving guests and which hallway was set aside for formal photos.

While the event took more than two months to plan the first time we catered it, since the event planner asked us to provide the exact same menu again, we saved a fair amount of prep work. Just the same, our kitchen staff took twenty hours to ready the hors d'oeuvres and the main course, and cleanup after the event occupied three full days. A party that size has a tendency to disrupt the overall process, so we're glad the smaller functions over the intervening two weeks have given us a chance to organize the kitchen again.

LESSONS/PROBLEMS

Many catering businesses can be swamped by all the cleaning and organizational tasks required to keep a kitchen in proper order. It's important to set aside designated times and days for duties, especially when you have a long break ahead of you. We like to assign each department head a specific list of things to do before everyone goes home.

PREDICTIONS

- *More general cleaning and organization*

DIARY

The day after Christmas is quiet, as one would expect. Our staff has been given the extended weekend off. But with my organizational and year-end responsibilities, I'm back in the kitchen for a few hours today.

We're anticipating a slow January, as is typical in this business. Our holiday rush extends from October through December, and wedding season runs from May through September. But January, February and March tend to be our slowest months as far as parties are concerned. That's one of the reasons I'm glad we have quite a few year-round contracts, since they serve to sustain us through the slow times. Another way we've increased business is by offering discounts to people who book parties by the end of December that are scheduled for the first three months of the next year. That strategy gives us a boost for February and March, so a slower January will be more palatable and perhaps even enjoyable before we prepare for the onslaught.

One of our contract clients is a literary arts organization. They bring in national authors to discuss their books and then offer a private reception for the attendees. For those of us who have caught the literature bug, it's a lot of fun to

JEFF FOCUSES ON THE STUFFED MUSHROOM PREP WORK.

work those receptions. Earlier this season we catered a lecture by Stephen King. As a writer I was incredibly excited by the prospect of meeting him, and I worked especially hard to make sure the food and the presentation were perfect. I found time to listen to him speak before we served, and his down-to-earth demeanor was pleasantly surprising. Unfortunately he was unable to attend the reception, but at least I had the chance to cater for one of my personal heroes.

I've found that running a catering business gives you many similar opportunities. I have mingled with a number of well-known people, including editor Frank Rich, novelist Frank McCourt, celebrity chef Caprial, and a handful of sports figures including members of the Portland Trailblazers basketball team and Seattle Mariners baseball team. While catering is sometimes thought to be a thankless career, it can open many doors you previously assumed were off-limits or unattainable.

In addition to the literary arts contract, we have our school lunches. Later this month I'll be meeting with administrators at other schools interested in adopting our program. A surprising number of schools in the area wish to provide healthier food to their students. We're hoping at least one or two of them will come onboard for the new school year that starts in the fall.

This afternoon we're also preparing for two upcoming New Year's events. We're especially looking forward to the surprise birthday party, since the honoree is one of our favorite repeat customers. We started working with Ana nearly three years ago, right after we opened for business, and she has faithfully continued to recommended us for many additional events. Oftentimes we find ourselves passed around within a circle of event-loving friends. We truly enjoy working with our repeat customers, and we strive to take extra steps to thank them for their loyalty.

Our standard preparation is underway for these last two parties of the year—confirming the menu and delivery options with the client, verifying the menu with our kitchen, reserving the necessary rental items through our local vendor, and coordinating the delivery day packet. In this packet are detailed instructions for our delivery staff including a map to the location and any specific customer requests, such as, "It's a surprise, so don't park in front of the house." We also enclose the client's contact information and a copy of the final invoice. The delivery folder we keep in our van contains sample menus and business cards, since our presence at a party invariably motivates guests to inquire about our services.

In addition to the party prep, today we're finalizing the details for next semester's school lunch program. As anticipated, we've received quite a few messages from frantic parents who are worried about signing up their children in time. There are always a few stragglers, especially right after Christmas when people start paying attention again to life's day-to-day activities. My assistant gladly accepts the task of responding to these last-minute requests to come up with a final count for our kitchen.

At the end of the day we're happy to head home. Before we leave there's a quick run-through of tomorrow's activities—do the payroll, calculate the year's receipts and confirm the week's food order—and then we're off, another successful day on the books.

LESSONS/PROBLEMS

We anticipated having last-minute lunch program registrations, and everyone was dealt with accordingly. Our priority for the rest of the week will be to finalize details for our January events and ensure our staff is well rested and recuperated for the start of the New Year

LET THE STUFFING BEGIN!

Day 6 | **DECEMBER 27**

PREDICTIONS

- *Cater a surprise birthday party for thirty guests*
- *Help out in the kitchen*

DIARY

Today, we have a surprise birthday party for thirty guests. This event is small enough to allow our regular kitchen staff to continue enjoying the holiday break. That means I'll be stepping into the kitchen to assist with the food preparation. The menu is comprised of crab-and-parmesan phyllo cups, sage-and-garlic-stuffed mushrooms, Thai peanut chicken skewers, and prawn cocktails.

My kitchen tasks for the day include washing and prepping the mushrooms, making the phyllo cups, and mixing the dips and sauces. All my professional experience up until now has involved marketing and advertising, except for a few stints as a restaurant hostess. I've really enjoyed honing my kitchen skills, and I try to pay attention to the chef when he explains how to core a tomato or properly slice up vegetables. My efforts here have significantly improved my kitchen skills at home, since I now find myself more comfortable with the whole meal preparation concept.

After washing and coring the mushrooms I work on sautéing the stuffing mix, which is a combination of garlic and onions that will later be mixed with sage and finely chopped mushroom stems. Once the sautéed mixture is cooked, we wrap it carefully and place it in the refrigerator to cool. Then I mix together the ingredients for our Thai peanut sauce and place it in the fridge as well. Though our chef is very particular about his menu items, an extra set of hands in the kitchen makes things run more smoothly and helps reduce the stress level.

The phyllo cups tend to be more labor-intensive than most things on our menu. By its very nature, phyllo dough is tricky to manipulate; it falls apart all too easily. In the early stages of my kitchen training I ruined more than my share of phyllo cups, but luckily our chef is a very understanding guy. Nowadays I'm able to make them on my own, including cutting the phyllo pastry into small squares, placing those squares into mini-muffin tins, stuffing them with the crab-

and-parmesan mix, and making sure I don't bake them too long.

Once my kitchen duties are complete, I start to gather our party items on the loading dock. I consult the kitchen checklist to make sure nothing is left out of the packing process. Tongs, chafing dishes, Sterno cans for warming and rental items—everything must be double-checked. We're careful to note the quantity of each item packed to guarantee nothing is left behind after we've finished catering the event. It's easy for silverware, serving utensils and napkins to go missing, so the checklist is often our most valuable possession.

Today's surprise party includes a number of rental items, such as tables, linens and folding chairs. Since it's a small event we're able to transport everything on our own. However, for larger ones, we often ask the rental place to handle the delivery and retrieval, often an after-hours excursion. Whenever possible we try to manage the rentals ourselves, as we've had some difficulty with deliveries in the past. One event several years ago took place about an hour north of town. Expecting 150 people, we needed a large number of things—15 tables, 150 chairs, and an equivalent quantity of linens, china and silverware. We were horrified when the truck was late. After numerous phone calls to the rental company manager, the truck was finally located and the driver given the proper directions. Thanks to a number of volunteer assistants we were able to set up the dining area in time, only to discover we were short quite a few chairs and linens, plus the plug-in soup kettle we'd reserved was inoperable. We frantically found an extra chafing dish in our van and served the soup in a rather non-conventional manner. We were also able to borrow chairs from the company next door, and the luncheon went off without any further hitches. The client was hardly pleased with the turn of events, even though we made sure to apologize profusely before cleaning things up and returning to our kitchen. Much to our delight, we were contacted the next year to cater the same event.

In addition to assembling the catering equipment, I always make sure the driver has explicit directions to the location—maps as well as written, turn-by-turn instructions—in addition to a stack of business cards and a final invoice for the client. Many of our customers pay by credit card, and I always include copies of the receipt with the final invoice. The food is the last thing we pack into the delivery van, and then I remind the driver to call me if he loses his way.

It's been a long year, and we're glad to see the last of it. Both the chef and I suffered through some difficult personal events, which made it tough to keep our chins up and continue with our regular business. We withdrew from a number of regular gigs because of that, which gave us the time to work through things. Even though running this business can sometimes be a pain, I'm grateful for the flexibility and the ability to focus on personal moments when necessary. And so I say, "Good riddance to 2006. Here's to a better year in 2007!"

LESSONS/PROBLEMS

In thinking about this past year, it's important to remember that life and work should be two separate worlds. As an owner, especially during our first few years in the business, I found myself consumed with work at home during my off-hours. It's important to differentiate between the two, or you'll never get any rest. As someone once told me, good fences make good neighbors, both in life and in work.

JEFF PROMISED ME I'D NEVER HAVE TO WORK IN A CUBICLE AGAIN.

Day 7 | *JANUARY 2*

PREDICTIONS

- *Begin this semester's school lunch program*
- *Finalize details for a rescheduled catering*
- *Get back in gear for the New Year*

DIARY

After the New Year, we return to a pile of dishes in a dirty kitchen. We catered two events over the weekend—the surprise birthday party and a New Year's Eve party—and our staff chose not to put in any extra cleaning time on New Year's Day. As a result, today is catch-up day. Our kitchen crew is busy scraping dishes, washing pots and pans, and wrapping clean items for use in future jobs. Once our equipment is clean we polish the silverware and the chafing dishes, wrapping them carefully in plastic film. That's how we keep everything pristine, even during long-term storage. You never want to take a stack of dusty glasses to an event.

A number of voice mail and e-mail messages were left for us over the holiday weekend. My assistant and I try to clear our desks by noon, returning calls and organizing files for the New Year. Three telephone messages involve weddings set for this summer. We can expect to receive wedding requests as much as a year ahead of the reception date, but January and February are especially busy since many couples get engaged during the holidays. That excitement translates into eager brides anxious to start planning their nuptials.

Because the previous fiscal year has just ended, it's also time for us to gather up our bookkeeping data for tax time in April. Many jurisdictions have their own requirements for the filing of business taxes, so we designed an office calendar that specifically tracks tax submission deadlines for city, county, and state filings. For instance, our county requires us to provide data on the value of our equipment, and a small percentage is levied against the cost of items purchased over the past year. My assistant heads to the kitchen, where she'll make a list of those acquisitions for this year's county tax assessment.

Meanwhile I'm in my office, sorting through receipts. One of the largest stacks is for last year's food purchases. Because we finally reached the stage where we have regular purveyors, the number of separate companies we buy from is smaller than in previous years. Our chef has been on top of his game throughout the year, keeping track of monthly expenditures. After an hour of double-checking his numbers, he proudly presents the kitchen expense list to me—a report broken down month by month—and I add it to my growing pile of data.

On the bookkeeping side, I make sure bank statements match the check register and can be tied to specific receipts. Our accounting software shows me the numbers are right on track, fully consistent with our annual projection. We monitor a number of expenditure categories including office equipment, kitchen equipment, advertising, membership fees, licensing, vehicle costs, and payroll. Considering we have twenty-seven staff members, using a local payroll company makes that part of the tax issue easy to handle. They keep track of unemployment insurance, total wages paid and worker's compensation contributions, sending us a single, easy-to-understand report that's included with the package I send to our accountant.

If you're running a business you need to do so intelligently, which means making good plans. It's important to draw up annual earnings projections and use that information to create realistic budgets for expenditures. With multiple purchases made throughout the year, especially for high-cost equipment, it's all too easy to go over budget. We also make sure to outsource those departments that can't be handled in-house, such as the accounting and payroll tasks. It's important to place people in roles that suit them best, and we've been very pleased with our decision to outsource those two responsibilities rather than trying to manage them ourselves.

I use the pile of receipts I've compiled to build an annual report that goes to our accountant. Many different documents get sent to a number of different offices at different times throughout the first three months of the year. We designed a color-coded system with folders labeled for city, county and state entities. The annual report we put together for our accountant is necessary for city and county offices as well. Our first due date is for a sales tax payment to the state of Washington, which is where we're incorporated. It pleases me to know I'm sending it out well ahead of schedule. Penalties are levied for late submissions, and I consider those penalties a serious waste of money. If you have the money, why not pay those bills early?

LESSONS/PROBLEMS

Our only problem today involved expenditure receipts. Even though we have a central location and file everything in one place, it can sometimes take us an extra hour just to track down receipts that aren't consistent with our accounting software or check register. It's important to ensure that everything matches across the board, or else you run the risk of offending three separate government entities: city, county and state. When starting a business, you have to make sure to fully comprehend which tax materials are due for submission, and when. Otherwise you may miss an important deadline and end up paying a financial penalty.

PREDICTIONS

- *Meet with a potential school client*
- *Do an event walk-through*

DIARY

Today is very meeting-intensive. In the morning I'm visiting with representatives from a local private school with an interest in our school lunch program for both students and faculty. I quickly gather up the paperwork I'll need and head downstairs to our meeting room to greet the school's director of development and a parent from their PTA. The discussion is pleasant, and I find both women bubbly and full of personality. You really never know what sort of meeting it will be until you sit down with the prospective client. Quite often the people who interview us already have a menu in mind, or else they're sold on hiring us even before we get together. That kind of positive energy is hard to beat. A number of aspects of our company make us stand out from the competition—our emphasis on organic and natural foods, our earth-friendly recycling practices, and our commitment to compost unusable leftovers and donate edible ones to local homeless shelters. These women seem truly excited about what we offer, and we're equally excited to provide them with such wonderful meals.

My meeting wraps up in less than an hour, after which the chef and I convene in my office to review my notes and dis-

I'M READY FOR A MEETING OR TASTING AT A MOMENT'S NOTICE!

cuss our ability to deliver what these folks want. This school client would triple our current lunch load. In addition, their students don't eat in a central cafeteria, so lunches would have to be delivered to individual classrooms every day, requiring a great deal of staff. Once we deliver the meals, we'll need our employees to stick around and assist with the cleanup before returning to the school's kitchen and then bring everything back here.

After discussing these complex logistics, the chef points out such a huge jump in participants not only would require more workers and delivery vehicles, but also additional kitchen equipment, refrigeration space and food storage space. Once we start to crunch the numbers—multiplying the number of participants by the price each student will pay, and then subtracting out the cost of additional staff and equipment—it becomes apparent all too quickly that giving this new lunch program the green light would be a losing proposition for us financially. At this point I'm tasked with relaying our decision back to the client, and then we move on to prepping for our next event.

One aspect of running a company is to know when to accept business and when to turn it away. Ever since opening our doors we've come to know other local business owners, and we're seeing both success and failure. It's important to recognize when seemingly wonderful assignments may be out of your league. It doesn't mean they'll always be out of reach, but it's vital to take care when contemplating growth. Be sure to know your strengths as well as your boundaries. Just as often, when you say no to one project, another one that fits you even better comes along. It's better to be a smart business owner than an out-of-business business owner!

Our chef heads downstairs to begin preparations for tomorrow's event for a group of local entrepreneurs. We're very excited about it, since we enjoy networking with other startups. This one will feature a number of celebrity entrepreneurs, and I'm anxious to meet them all. We find that fellow entrepreneurs are often our most vocal supporters, passing around our cards to their friends and inviting us to cater additional events.

Today's preparation includes a quick walkthrough of the event location, so off I go to check it out. Upon arriving I'm greeted by a local party planner with whom we work on a regular basis. She always has such terrific energy, and today is no exception. The event space is set up with tables and chairs, and our two buffet locations are marked out in opposite corners of the room. One thing I notice right away, however, is that the floor seems cramped for the number of tables and chairs in place. I sense our staff will have difficulty crossing the room once it's packed with people, and I make note of my concern to discuss later with our chef. As always happens in the catering business, it's about being able to adjust quickly. Having an event plan is vital, but having a backup or alternative plan is just as important. I mention to the event planner that the space seems cramped. While she agrees, it doesn't seem to concern her. "We'll just have to see how it goes," she says, just before I jump in my car and head back to the kitchen. Yes, we'll have to see how it goes—and we'll make sure to have Plan B ready to implement.

LESSONS/PROBLEMS

The only significant problem we had today was determining whether the new school lunch program would be feasible for us. It's important to discuss the logistics of a new project before deciding whether to take it on. Despite our interest in expansion, it's vital not to move too quickly or to say yes to something that's larger than you can deliver. Growing too fast can kill an enterprise just as fast as a lack of business.

OUR BUFFET IS READY TO GO.

Day 9 | *JANUARY 4*

PREDICTIONS

- *Pay our first-of-the-month bills*
- *Prep and cater the entrepreneurs' party*

DIARY

Today is our event for the local entrepreneur group, so we arrive at the kitchen by 8:00 A.M., following a quick stop for coffee. Most of our initial kitchen preparation has already been completed, so today's responsibilities include finalizing the menu items, assembling the catering and rental equipment, and working the event itself. We're scheduled to depart the kitchen by 4:00 P.M., with the event running from 5:00 to 9:00. We already know it's scheduled to be a four-

A QUICK STAFF PHOTO BEFORE THE CHAOS BEGINS.

teen-hour day today, so we give a collective sigh and then set off on our individual tasks.

With plenty of kitchen staff on hand I'll spend my day in the office, since they won't need me to help out down there. It's time to pay the bills and finish up payroll. When I sit down at my desk, I see a note from my assistant that recounts a difficult phone call she had yesterday afternoon. We have a new client interested in ordering box lunches for his office. As of a year ago we instituted a minimum order threshold, and he is apparently unhappy with that requirement. Since we have quite a few regular lunch contracts to fulfill, we increased our minimum so as to not overload our staff with smaller lunch parties during the school year; for example, those with fifteen or fewer guests. Parties of this size cause us to barely break even from a profitability perspective, so it's best to turn that business away. I make a quick phone call to this gentleman and explain our situation, telling him we'd be happy to discuss multiple event bookings in order to meet the minimum. He is not amenable to this suggestion and instead elects to go with another caterer. You can't make everyone happy all the time!

While I'm in the office preparing the weekly payroll and paying this month's bills, the kitchen is humming away. Today's party includes a number of fresh hors d'oeuvres and my favorite dessert item on our menu, Zen Bananas. Tonight, in addition to exposing our food and services to 150 potential clients, I also have the honor of attending as a guest. Instead of helping to replenish the buffet, I'll actually get to enjoy it! As a caterer you can work up to twenty hours on an event, and then watch others enjoy the fruits of your labor. After spending all that time and effort preparing an extensive menu, you're often too tired of the kitchen and end up at the closest fast-food establishment for dinner. It's a terrible cycle in our industry, but a common one. I take a break from my office duties and lend a hand with the equipment organization and the delivery van loading. Then it's time to change into my party dress. Tonight I'll enjoy being a business owner.

The location for tonight's event is only ten blocks from the office, which will ease our pain if we need to retrieve something we've forgotten during the load-in process. Within minutes of our arrival our staff begins stacking the food and beverages into the back kitchen, while the chef and I head

SOME OF OUR FAVORITE HORS D'OEUVRES.

for the main room to discuss strategy with the event planner. An hour later, a steady stream of guests has begun to arrive. The buffet is set up and the bars are humming smoothly, but we've had to do a bit of shuffling behind the scenes because one of our staff members failed to show. When planning an event, I always confirm dates, times and locations with our workers the day before. While we occasionally have someone out sick or delayed for a personal reason, we rarely have staff members that simply don't show up. However, in a strange turn of events, one of our unscheduled employees happens to arrive, and we quickly press him into service. Sometimes the universe works with you instead of against you.

The evening begins to swing, and it quickly becomes apparent that the venue is proving too small for the number of

THE EVENT LOCATION BEFORE THE ROOM FILLED TO CAPACITY.

attendees. Guests are finding it difficult to get from one side of the room to the other, while a large group has clogged up the center by parking themselves in plastic chairs to listen to the evening's guest speakers. Even though I'm a guest tonight, I find myself stuck in my standard event mode, checking on buffet levels and keeping an eye on staff members. It's only when our chef removes a stack of dirty dishes from my hands and tells me to relax that I finally sit down to listen to a local celebrity chef discuss her start in the business.

Once her speech is over, I make a beeline to introduce myself. A few guests have told me she enjoyed our buffet of hors d'oeuvres, so I'm looking forward to discussing food with her. Unfortunately she turns out to be a woman of very few words, and I'm left wondering if perhaps she's been so inundated with unfamiliar faces all evening long that all she wants to do is go home. I cut our conversation short and simply thank her for coming. Many guests have apparently picked up our business cards from the buffet table, and my weary staff looks happy that the evening has ended. We exchange joyous high-fives as the last guest walks out the door.

LESSONS/PROBLEMS
Having a party in a location unsuited for the event is a common mistake. It's important that the venue can comfortably hold the number of expected guests, and don't forget to factor in the amount of space you'll need for rented or display items. A stage or a dance floor can often make the difference between a great event and an all-too-short one.

PREDICTIONS

- *Clean-up from the entrepreneurs' party*
- *Place a food order*

DIARY

Except for our regularly scheduled school lunch, our only other task today involves cleaning. Last night's party went very well, with no major difficulties. Our food was well received and we made some good contacts in the local business community, including a wedding guide publisher. I'm a big fan of making the right contacts wherever we're serving.

We had planned on the correct guest count, so there's hardly any food left over. With all the items we rented for the evening, including china and barware, our dishwasher has his work cut out for him early this morning. Everything we rent needs to be rinsed before it's returned, so we try to get that task out of the way immediately. When I arrive at ten o'clock, I'm pleased to note our delivery driver is already on his way to return the rentals. It's good to see things running smoothly in my absence.

Our chef, looking a bit worse for wear, finds himself knee-deep in kitchen re-organization as well as updating the food inventory. Since it's the beginning of the month, we have a major food order to place. As caterers in a niche market, we have fewer options when it comes to food purveyors. Our primary supplier is a large distributor of organic and natural goods, and we're one of their rare caterer customers among the local grocery stores and co-ops they serve. Once inventory is finished, the chef can complete the food order and submit it online. Delivery will take place the following Monday during a very early four-hour window. Oh, the joys of running a business!

Today there's a pleasant tone in the kitchen. As owners we're pleased with last night's event, and the staff has been appropriately commended for their hard work. If we move things along today, we can all get out a little early and begin our weekends. Extra time for rest is always appreciated.

At 2:00 the chef and I sit down at my desk to work on the food order for next week. I'm responsible for keeping track of all non-food items, such as disposables, coffee, tea, and toilet paper. I add my items to his perishables and then we enter everything onto our supplier's Web-based order form. Our distributor keeps track of on-hand stock in real time, which is very helpful. The first several orders we placed with them, we panicked when things we'd selected didn't show up with the rest of our stuff. Now we make sure to check every item to avoid last-minute surprises due to manufacturer shortages.

Now that the food order is sent, my Friday responsibilities are completed. I take a few minutes to organize my desk for next week and then head out the door.

LESSONS/PROBLEMS

One of the best lessons for running a successful enterprise is to make great contacts. When we started this business, we joined a number of local networking groups. Even though you may meet people whose businesses are too small to hire you, many of them are happy to pass along your contact details to larger concerns. One such membership that's served us well is the local "green" business guide. Our ad in the guide is less expensive than a similar one in the Yellow Pages, and its distribution is aimed at people in the community most likely to hire us. In addition to our regular display ads, we also participate in their networking meetings and annual trade shows. Those are catering opportunities as well!

Another lesson to remember is that every event is an opportunity to advertise. I make sure we have plenty of business cards sitting on the buffet table. We've captured more business from people eating our food at a wedding or a meeting than we've ever had from responses to print ads. And instead of the industry-standard catering uniform—black trousers, white shirt and black tie—our staff wears mandarin-collared shirts embroidered with our logo. This not only makes us stand out in a crowd, it also causes guests to remember the company's name while they're enjoying our wonderful food.

PREDICTIONS

- *Receive a food order*
- *Start another school week*
- *Meet with management staff*

DIARY

Today we're expecting our monthly dry goods order and, as usual, we're having problems with the delivery. The company suggests we phone early in the morning to determine a delivery time. It seems we're often given the wrong time or told there will be a four-hour window in which to anticipate delivery. Since we're not like most places on their route and don't open at 6:00 A.M., this makes it difficult to figure out when to show up. This morning I'm told the delivery is scheduled for 9:00, but we decide to get there at 7:45, just in case. Barely ten minutes after we've left the house, the delivery driver calls me to say he's parked in front of our building and ready to drop off our order. Fortunately our lunch service manager has arrived early and is available to sign for everything. Upon arrival I review what's been delivered. We're a few items short, so I make note of them on the kitchen inventory sheet and on the supplier's order form. After putting everything away, I ring up the purveyor and make sure they credit our account for the non-delivered items. One task down, and many more to go!

Our management meeting this morning includes the chef,

PAM, OUR LUNCH MANAGER, GATHERS EVERYTHING NEEDED FOR THE DAY'S LUNCH SERVICE.

the lunch service manager, and the kitchen manager. Our first priority is to review what events are on our calendar this month. We have a number of recurring events, such as the school lunch program and standing box lunch orders for business meetings, plus there are a few parties for groups with fewer than 100 guests. I let everyone know I'm starting to get inquiries from wedding couples, and this summer looks to be a busy one. After reviewing our upcoming gigs we discuss details of last month's events, noting any issues we may have had with staffing, vehicles or food items.

Our lunch delivery person expresses some concerns she's having with the lunch service. We have two children signed up as vegetarians, but they appear to be more interested in eating the meat dishes than the vegetarian ones. We've come across this issue a few times before, where parents will check off "vegetarian" on the sign-up sheet simply because their child is a bit fussier than normal. After considerable discussion, we agree it's not our place to enforce eating regulations with these children, and instead we'll increase the number of meat servings we provide to include them. There will continue to be a vegetarian item available, but we'll bring fewer quantities to guarantee less waste.

Once our meeting has adjourned, I review e-mail and voice-mail messages received over the weekend. I have several meetings scheduled with couples planning wedding receptions. With a fairly full calendar planned for February and March, I need to take a closer look at hiring additional staff. I set aside some time in my schedule later this week to deal with that issue.

I receive several phone calls for events scheduled for the next few weeks. With the birth of our second child expected in May, I'm more likely to book as many events as possible prior to that. Even though the chef and I plan to work through the summer, as usual, I'd prefer to schedule a minimal number of events after May to spend some recovery time at home and enjoy our expanding family.

This week, in addition to meeting with wedding couples and organizing a new staff list, we've also been contacted about a small hors d'oeuvres event for Thursday, plus a box lunch delivery for this afternoon. When my office tasks have been completed for the morning, I head down to the kitchen to assist with the 25 box lunches due out shortly.

Our corporate client has ordered a number of gourmet items for these box lunches, including Asian shrimp wrap, grilled chicken Caesar wrap, and marinated steak fajita wrap. Our Asian shrimp wrap is my favorite, made with grilled and marinated shrimp, tangy red cabbage, and Thai chili sauce. The chef and I have worked out a deal when it comes to box lunch orders. If I help out in the kitchen, I get a box lunch for myself. Today I also offer to make the delivery downtown so I can spend some time window-shopping during my lunch hour.

LESSONS/PROBLEMS

Today's major issue involved our morning delivery. While we try to confirm a regular delivery time for our dry goods order, it's not always possible. Our staff works flexible hours with minimal overlapping time, which allows us to have people on hand to cover any last-minute schedule changes, like an unexpected early delivery. I always think ahead when planning the schedule, making sure to incorporate both kitchen and office staff into the overall shop responsibilities.

PREDICTIONS

- *Meet with couples planning wedding receptions*

DIARY

My schedule today includes meetings with two couples planning wedding receptions. The couple this morning will marry at Cannon Beach, a popular site on the Oregon coast. This afternoon's couple plans to hold their reception at a local spot called the Leach Botanical Gardens. Both appear to be small, intimate affairs, exactly the kind we like to cater.

My first meeting of the day is with Brenda and Jason. They're getting married in August, with their ceremony on the beach and their reception at a local community hall, a place we've worked a number of times before. They're expecting 100–150 guests, including a number of vegans and vegetarians. First, I explain they should anticipate that 80–85 percent of their guests will show up, although that can change depending on the number of local invitees as opposed to out-of-towners. Also, in the case of a "destination" wedding such as the coastal event they're planning, some guests will be unable to travel the distance or cover the costs of renting a hotel room. We recently catered a reception at this Cannon Beach community center, so I offer them a number of tips—for example, have umbrellas on hand to shade against the sun, and set up chairs on the beach to accommodate older guests. While they have a number of special dietary needs to address in the menu, I advise them to remember their out-of-town guests may not be familiar with vegan and vegetarian items.

They have decided on a vegan barbeque menu, with non-vegan items for meat-eaters. For starters we choose sage-and-garlic-stuffed mushrooms and a Mediterranean platter, lemon-pepper salmon plus marinated vegetable skewers as entrees, a sweet corn salad, red-potato salad, and chocolate-dipped strawberries. For dessert, they'll serve vegan cupcakes made at a local bakery. In addition to the food we compile a list of rental items, including enough chairs for the reception and the ceremony, linens, china, silverware, and glassware. There will also be bar service, so I put wine and pilsner glasses on the list. As with all our coastal events, we're responsible for transporting the rented goods to and from our local vendor, so we briefly discuss their additional delivery expenses. I promise to have a proposal in their hands within the next few days.

During the short break between meetings I sit with my office assistant to discuss any pressing needs. There are a few voice-mail and e-mail messages awaiting replies, a number of them donation requests for local charitable events. We've become well known in the community as regular donors, especially to non-profit organizations and educational groups. We have a standing dessert donation to the annual fund-raiser for a women's shelter, and we often contribute gift certificates for hors d'oeuvres parties to silent auctions and benefits. After discussing our current open donations, I recommend that my assistant return everyone's calls and assure them of our intention to donate. I find that even the smallest donation to a local organization receives plenty of recognition. Not only does it make us feel good, we're also giving to a great cause. It furthermore provides us with excellent exposure throughout the community and among people who will thereafter be inclined to hire us for their private events.

My next appointment is after lunch, so I go out to grab a quick bite. It's fun to check out what's being offered at other food service locations, so I try to visit various catering and restaurant facilities as often as I can. Today I venture into a local deli to pick up lunch, and I take a moment to look over their catering menu. I keep a stack of my competitors' menus at my desk and review them with our chef every few months. This keeps us on our toes, ensuring that we're offering popular items as well as our signature ones. After returning to my office I file the menu away for discussion at a later time.

Once two o'clock rolls around, I'm patiently waiting in our meeting room to visit with the next wedding couple. Unfortunately, the longer I sit and wait, the more I wonder if my meeting has been cancelled without notification. Not only does this happen to me when I'm interviewing for new staff members—which I need to do soon—it also takes place all too often when meeting with wedding couples. Oftentimes I'll receive a last minute e-mail or voice-mail from a frantic bride-to-be begging us to reschedule for a later date. After waiting thirty minutes, I head upstairs to see if there have been any messages from my delayed guests. Sure enough, e-mail is waiting for me to let me know the meeting had to be cancelled because of a delayed mother-in-law visit from out of town. Since a tasting was not part of our discussion, there's no food wasted and the rescheduled meeting is a minor offense. I let the nervous bride know next week will work just fine.

LESSONS/PROBLEMS

There was a minor problem with the absent couple in the afternoon. It's important to remain flexible, because you're dealing with people with busy schedules and fiancées and mothers-in-law. I take it all in stride and enjoy the break, since I never know when I'll see down time again in this crazy business.

LUNCH DOESN'T JUST HAPPEN BY ITSELF.

Day 13 | JANUARY 10

PREDICTIONS

- *Follow up on unpaid invoices*
- *Head home early*

DIARY

The meat purveyor we're expecting to show up this morning is running late. Then everything goes frantic when he finally does arrive, with all hands needed on deck to help unload and put the food items away. I decide to help with today's lunch preparation so our delivery drivers can get out the door in a timely manner. Today's menu is very child-friendly, including chicken soft tacos, black beans, and Spanish rice. I'm responsible for thawing the frozen chicken, slicing it into bite-sized cubes, and cooking it on the stove with the appropriate spices. While I work away, our dishwasher gets busy cleaning the recently used lunch equipment, and our delivery person starts to pack up the van.

I came to this business with no previous experience in kitchen work, and I've learned a great many things since then. As required by the state of Oregon, I have a food handler's card that allows me to step in whenever I'm needed, whether here in the kitchen or out on our catering runs. This tends to help a great deal, especially when staff members are sick or late to work, or simply when an extra pair of hands is needed.

As a certified food handler I'm required to know the rules and regulations regarding both in-house and off-site preparation. It's important to be aware of proper food-storage and food-serving temperatures when running a food service business of any kind. More than once we've arrived at our facility to find a surprise visitor in our midst, the county health inspector. Since all our staff members are fully licensed and no one works here without an updated food handler's card, our kitchen is generally in good order when it comes to state regulations. In addition, we make sure to advise our staff as often as necessary when it comes to rules being stretched or broken, such as the one declaring, "No drinking on the food line." A surprising number of people in this business are smokers, and our chef is adamant about multiple hand-washings before any of them returns to the kitchen. Who wants to eat something smelling of cigarettes?

THE VAN IS LOADED WITH TRAYS, SILVERWARE, HOT FOOD, AND BEVERAGES.

An hour later, once the lunch van has left for its deliveries, it's time to deal with my office responsibilities. We assembled all our tax information for last year and sent it along to our accountant, so that weight is off my shoulders. Today I need to deal with any unpaid invoices hanging around from events we catered in 2006. There's only one outstanding invoice this year, which makes my job easier. Last year we started asking for payment in full seven business days prior to an event. That way we're not financing someone's food orders, and the client doesn't have to worry about paying the bill when we show up, when they may be worried about other things. Weddings have always been paid ahead of time, but we've found that our customers appreciate not having to track down their checkbook or dig out their credit card while entertaining their guests.

In many corporate settings, however, there are often multiple people who must be consulted before a check can be issued. As a result, we'll bill them with the expectation of receiving payment within the week. The key is to make sure no one takes advantage of you, which can happen, and that a late payment won't break you.

This year's sole outstanding invoice is for a local corporation that, unfortunately, has earned a reputation for not paying its vendors. In fact, my newspaper-reading grandmother had warned me not to do business with them. But the party was a small one, so I'm hopeful it won't take much coercing to get our money. Three weeks have passed since the event, and I've e-mailed my contact there several times. I decide to call the woman's supervisor. I receive the same run-around answers regarding delays in the billing department, at which point I mention we'd be happy to resolve this issue in small claims court. Apparently this suggestion seems to resonate with someone at the corporate office. Within minutes of hanging up the phone she calls me back with a credit card number. "We'll just charge the balance due," she offers. Sometimes you have to be willing to play hardball to get the job done.

LESSONS/PROBLEMS

I anticipated a problem today with the outstanding invoice. I'm always amazed when even large corporations try to escape their financial responsibilities, and you have to be ready to handle those situations quickly and professionally. Small claims court should always be a last resort, but it remains an option for any business owner who's trying to get paid for services rendered.

PREDICTIONS

- *Poor weather may cause us some delays*
- *Work from home*

DIARY

The city awakens to a new layer of snow on the ground. Snow is unusual in the Portland area, so it's quite a sight. But for those of us in the food delivery business, it can mean treacherous driving and rescheduled events. We phone the schools early to determine who's closed and who's open. While the area's public schools have already announced closures, our clients are small, private entities and have elected to hold classes. Since private schools rely more on parents than school buses for student transportation, they often remain open under these circumstances. I elect to work from home, so I wish Jeff well as he heads out the door to look after today's catering responsibilities.

I'm amazed that we've hardly had any events affected by the weather over the past four years. Most of those were weddings out on the Oregon coast, where a sudden rainstorm can surprise everyone. I usually try to dissuade couples wanting to schedule a beach wedding there in the fall, since doing so can be tempting fate. Over the past year we catered four coastal weddings, with two in Cannon Beach, one in Astoria, and one in Yachats. Both Cannon Beach weddings took place in mid-September, and both of them suffered rain. It was good that the receptions were held indoors, and we had hot coffee and tea waiting for the drenched guests when they arrived for dinner. We try to stay abreast of weather conditions regardless of the event we're catering, just so we can anticipate potential difficulties.

I decide it's time to review our staffing needs for the upcoming year. Every quarter, especially once we're past our busy time, I look over our personnel list to determine which workers to keep on and which to jettison. Our regular ten staff members have been wonderful to work with over the past few months, although I know several of them are full-time students and may have scheduling conflicts in the upcoming quarter. I employ a two-step process in this regard. First I determine which people we'd like to stay on. I make sure to have meetings with my management team, where we all provide our assessments. Once we've determined the serving staff we'd like to keep, I e-mail everyone, asking them if they wish to remain on our event phone list. Since our staffing people are part-timers, employees occasionally leave due to more pressing duties, whether a full-time job or responsibilities at home. We're always sure to let the good ones decide whether they want to stay or not. Once our current staff members have responded to my request, I try to plan for the number of staffers we'll actually need over the next few months. Only two hours after I send out my e-mails today, eight of the ten staffers have already responded. Six elect to remain on our call list, while the other two ask to be removed. This means I'll need to hire from two to four staff members this quarter.

I like to save money by placing online ads with a local bulletin board server. We've had mixed success with this bulletin board, but it's free so it's a good place to start. College students and stay-at-home parents, ideal demographics for us, check these listings regularly. We require outgoing, friendly staff members easily reached by telephone and e-mail, and people who have reliable transportation and a flexible schedule. Staff members are also required to possess an Oregon food handler's card before they apply. They must also have at least two to three years of catering experience—preferably banquet staffing—and possess an appreciation of organic and natural foods. While our requirements may sound too specific, we've had some bad experiences in the past with people lacking reliable transportation or the requisite background in the catering and banquet business. It makes sense for us to start with the right staff from the beginning, rather that finding out later someone is a poor fit.

In addition to the bulletin board posting, I shoot an e-mail message to my friend at a local culinary school. We love having culinary students work for us, since they generally possess a better understanding of the whole food service process, and our hours often fit nicely into their schedules. We have event staff apportioned regarding daytime and evening events, so if our full-time job staffers happen to be unavailable during the day, we have a list of those who can service morning and early afternoon events, and the same for evenings.

LESSONS/PROBLEMS

Our problem today was the weather, which can't be avoided no matter how hard you try. Although terrible weather comes rarely to the Portland area, it's important to be prepared with a staffing back-up plan. I like to have a list of local staffers handy who can step in and carry out the day's responsibilities, in case our regularly scheduled staffers are unable to make it in. It's just as important to recognize when the weather is just too severe to cater an event at all. It's helpful to have a weather clause as part of your catering contracts, just in case. After all, if the caterer can't make it through the snow, it's unlikely the partygoers will get there either.

PREDICTIONS

- *Reschedule a wedding couple*

DIARY

My responsibilities today include reviewing resumes for prospective hires and meeting with a wedding couple this morning—the same pair who rescheduled from last week. I arrive at the kitchen around nine o'clock and start by checking the voice-mail and e-mail messages left this past weekend. Several individuals have called to ask for quotes on events for the late spring and summer, so my assistant takes over and starts to call them back with the information they've requested.

The wedding couple arrives at ten o'clock. Janelle and Aaron are planning a June wedding at a local arboretum called Leach Botanical Gardens. It's a beautiful location with plenty of walking trails, a central mansion, and garden space ideal for wedding ceremonies and receptions. We catered our very first wedding at Leach and everything went splendidly. We enjoy working with the staff there, so we're looking forward to visiting Leach again this summer.

Janelle doesn't have any particular concerns other than a mild level of stress related to the wedding plans in general. Most of their guests live around town, and no one has yet expressed any special dietary needs. Their guest list numbers between 80 and 100, and they're interested in having "passed" hors d'oeuvres for the reception. We refer to this as "butlered hors d'oeuvres," and while we add a per-person charge for this service, some clients would rather have food items offered directly to their guests rather than forcing them to queue up in a buffet line. This allows everyone to mingle without confining them to a more structured environment. They're planning a formal, late-afternoon reception that will run into the early evening, with black-and-white attire and decor, so butlered service will go quite nicely here.

This couple has pre-selected most of what they want, which makes our meeting go faster. I'm surprised by the number of people who visit us without first reviewing our menus. When contacting potential clients I always suggest they look over our material, either sent to them as an e-mail attachment or found on our Web site, in order to get a better understanding of our services and selections. I enjoy meeting clients at any stage in their planning, but these meetings are much more successful if the menu has been reviewed and the clients are familiar with what we offer.

The menu they've chosen for this wedding reception includes double-cream French-baked Brie with roasted garlic, marinated vegetables, sage-and-garlic-stuffed mushrooms, Thai peanut chicken skewers, and wild mushroom pot-stickers. These last items are a wonderful combination of green onion mixed with Portobello and Crimini mushrooms, served with a soy-and-chili dipping sauce. As with all our weddings I recommend the chocolate-covered strawberries. These tend to be a wonderful compliment to any wedding cake and serve equally well as a stand-alone dessert, should the wedding couple decide not to have cake.

In addition to the butlered food menu, Aaron and Janelle also want an open bar. After running our own bar during the first few years we were open, now we contract out that portion of the business to a local bartending service. They're specialists in this aspect of the service industry, and it also removes us from state licensing and insurance concerns when providing alcoholic beverages to the public.

One of our topics of discussion is a basic timeline of the day of the event, including how long we'll take to set everything up, where and when the wedding ceremony will take place and how long it's expected to last, at what time we should begin serving the food and opening the bar, and where the cake-cutting ceremony falls. Oftentimes couples planning a wedding ceremony and reception haven't thought about these details, and discussing them with me seems to aid their overall focus. As our meeting comes to a close, I thank Aaron and Janelle for coming and make sure they know I'll have a proposal to them within a few days. I also point out that they're welcome to contact me via telephone or e-mail with any questions or concerns.

When it comes to wedding couples, we often end up playing wedding counselors along with our role of providing food and beverages for the event. Planning a wedding can be very stressful, especially if there are difficulties between families. At one of our weddings a summer or two ago, the mother of the bride and the mother of the groom did not get along. The bride's side was responsible for the wedding reception while the groom's side provided the rehearsal dinner, scheduled for the evening before the ceremony. We were hired to cater both events and planning was a bit tricky, since neither mother wanted to be in the same room with the other. That put an awful lot of stress on the bride, and I found myself comforting her as she cried during one of our planning meetings. Because most couples are first-time wedding planners themselves, the stress of trying to handle everything is a significant challenge. I find myself stepping away from the role of traditional caterer and offering compassion and understanding as much as advice on which wines to serve with dinner.

Because of all my other duties—phone calls, meetings and proposals—I don't have time to review job resumes today. Sometimes my pre-planned schedule doesn't go as hoped, but it's important to handle more important items as they come up and leave the remaining tasks for another day.

LESSONS/PROBLEMS

I truly enjoyed meeting that couple today, but the bride seemed a bit stressed out to me. Though it's not always stereotypical of a bride and groom, you have to learn when to offer your assistance to those who are not used to planning large events. I always try to reassure my clients that I'm here to help them any way I can, even if that advice is not necessarily directly related to the catering aspect of the event.

PREDICTIONS

- *Deal with weather issues*
- *Focus on staffing and hiring*

DIARY

Due to a sudden snowstorm in the Portland area we're late getting to the office. Because snowfall in the city is unusual, when it shows up the whole town seems to grind to a halt. Having grown up in Michigan, a small amount of snow doesn't bother me. We make it to the office in plenty of time. Many of the area's schools are closed for the day, but our client is open so the kitchen must remain active. Once we arrive at the shop, Jeff heads to the kitchen to begin his lunch-prep routine. Meanwhile, I plan to concentrate on the resumes we've received so far, since I didn't get to them yesterday. I posted a request for staffers on a local online bulletin board and also distributed this inquiry to several local culinary programs. After a week we've received close to sixty resumes via e-mail and fax, and I sit down at my desk to sort through them.

It's been an interesting experience for me as a business owner. Even though I receive a large number of resumes every time I place a job posting, I'm surprised at how few of these respondents are actually qualified for the positions we're trying to fill. Many will claim that serving experience isn't all that important, but we truly want to hire people familiar with banquets and catering. That old adage, "serving is serving," gets bandied about a lot in the food service industry, but working as a caterer is a whole lot different than being a waiter. In a restaurant you deal with individual tables and individual orders, providing a complete restaurant experience that includes discussing the day's specials, taking everyone's order, delivering food to the table, and processing payment. In catering the menu is already decided, so one is usually concerned with replenishing buffet items and busing dirty dishes and silverware. With butlered or plated events, there's a real skill involved in delivering food items efficiently and politely.

We've had problems in the past with servers who lacked catering experience. In several of our early plated events we missed serving tables or delivered the wrong item to the wrong person. In one instance our serving staff passed by an entire table of VIPs, including the woman who hired us for the event. Needless to say, she was not happy about that. Now we have very explicit requirements for the hiring process, which makes the overall procedure much more thorough. Conventional wisdom states that satisfied customers tell five friends about their great experience, but dissatisfied ones will spread the word to as many as twenty acquaintances. People tend to remember bad service more often than good. In a small town like Portland, it only takes a few of those situations and you're out of business.

Today, somewhere around half of the responses I've received have little to no catering experience, so those resumes go directly into the shredder. More than a dozen of these people have no serving experience of any kind. I realize this is a part-time gig, but you'd think folks would understand you need at least some experience to do this job. In the past I've received resumes from environmental scientists, nurses, marketing managers, and even police officers. Another lesson we've learned is to make note of those who've owned a catering business in the past or show a particularly high level of interest in how we operate. We've hired servers who took what they learned from working for us and used that knowledge to open their own catering business as direct competitors. While I admire the entrepreneurial spirit, I find this to be a very sneaky way of showing it. It's not that we're in possession of deep corporate secrets. I simply want to hire friendly, capable people who aren't here to steal our business.

I'm left with eight interview candidates out of 60 respondents. If past experience is any indication, I imagine only two or three will be offered a job. Hiring people is one of my least favorite parts of owning a business, but it's a necessary evil.

LESSONS/PROBLEMS

It was tedious to weed through all the resumes we received from people looking to fill our server positions. The hiring process is an incredibly important one for any business, but even more so when your staff occupies the front line of service. It pays to be extra fussy about your staff in every area of the catering operation. Bad service equals bad business, and bad business can ultimately lead to being out-of-business!

PREDICTIONS

- *Wrestle with additional weather-related difficulties*
- *Prepare for Friday's event*

DIARY

We had another snowstorm overnight and our school lunch program is shut down for the day, as is most of the city. Fortunately I'm primed to work from home, so it's business as usual except for the fact that our chef is fast asleep at a time when he's normally doing kitchen prep work. When we first started our business I worked from home most of the time. During those first few months we shared a kitchen with another caterer, so there was no room for me to have an office there. I enjoyed going to work in my pajamas every morning! But even after our move to a building with space for an office, my previous experience made it easier for me to adapt when logistical issues like bad weather or power outages arose. From my home office I have full access to our business files plus e-mails and faxes, so the transition becomes seamless.

I take a quick moment to forward all telephone calls from the office phone to here, and I check with our school client to confirm that classes are indeed cancelled. For some reason I'm paranoid about having received incorrect data, so I have a habit of double- and even triple-checking these things. It may sound crazy, but it only takes one big mistake—like showing up on the wrong day or driving to the wrong location—before you have that little voice in the back of your mind calling on you to confirm and re-confirm every event, big or small.

I spend most of my morning returning phone calls regarding potential catering jobs. We have a large job coming up Friday evening, with more than 150 guests expected, so after those calls are made I work on finalizing details for that event. We're catering a silent auction fundraiser for a local nonprofit group, our fourth time working with them. We enjoy doing things on the local nonprofit scene, especially when these organizations support causes we believe in. This association is involved with conserving wildlife and preserving the environment—things we feel strongly about as individuals and as a business—so we're happy to support them any way we can.

It's been an exciting event for us to cater every year. They were thrilled to find us, having sought a caterer of organic food for a long time. The first time we worked this event was back when Jeff and I were running the show pretty much by ourselves, and we had two other caterings booked that day. We arrived at the location with our serving staff to discover the building situated on a main downtown street with no loading zone. On top of that, the building was hosting two other catered events beside the one we were working, and all three catering companies plus invited guests were forced to use the same slow elevator. Needless to say, it taught us to do our homework and scout out locations ahead of time.

The two most recent events have taken place at a ballroom barely two blocks from our kitchen, which makes our job considerably easier. The menu has remained the same each year—entrees of pesto-encrusted wild salmon plus stuffed bell peppers for the vegans and vegetarians, herb-roasted red potatoes, tossed field greens, and an assortment of brownies and cookies for dessert. The ballroom has its own supply of tables and chairs, so our responsibilities are limited to food, linens and place settings. I love it when catering jobs are this easy.

Shortly after lunch I check with our contact at the ballroom to inquire about last-minute changes. She tells me the guest count remains the same and nothing else has changed. The host will provide the alcoholic beverages, and our bartending contractor is looking after the service. At this point the event has become much like a pair of favorite shoes, familiar and comfortable without any last-minute surprises.

Then it's time to call the rental company and confirm that our order has been received for tonight's event. While we stock a small quantity of linens and china, we leave large quantities and the question of varied designs and colors to the professionals. Everything seems to be in order, so that's one less thing for me to worry about. My next task is to finish writing the proposals for the two wedding couples I met with this past week. Both are fairly simple, and I'm finished with the details within a few hours. I send these to each respective couple as e-mail attachments and grab a few minutes to enjoy a quick snack on the couch in front of the television. Naturally the office phone rings during my break, so I run back to the office to help the next client with a catering proposal. There's hardly a moment when I can afford to rest on my laurels.

LESSONS/PROBLEMS

The weather was a mess today, so we made some quick judgments and rearranged a few things. Catering can be a surprising business in the truest sense of the word, with last-minute events, last-minute changes and last-minute issues. Flexibility is vital, and it helps to anticipate any problems that might arise. As soon as we learned the weather was deteriorating, we called our staff members the night before to bring them up to date on our plans and expectations. I also made sure to bring home whatever files I figured I might need, just in case the snowstorm was as bad as predicted—which it was.

ERIC KEEPS AN EYE ON THE BUFFET AND ANSWERS ANY QUESTIONS THAT GUESTS MIGHT HAVE.

Day 18 | *JANUARY 19*

PREDICTIONS

- *Still more weather issues*
- *Prepare for tonight's event*

DIARY

It's event day and the kitchen is already rocking by the time we arrive at 8:00 A.M. The snowstorm has put a damper on the entire city. Our school client is closed again, the fourth day in the row. However, tonight's event will go on come rain or shine—or snow!

While the kitchen works its way through the food preparation list, my assistant and I gather up the front-of-the-house materials we'll need. A checklist designed from the details of the proposal that went to the client was used to build our initial packing list. Part of that information includes the guest count, so we'll know which and how many of each item to pull from our own inventory. I send my assistant to pick up the rental items while I hunt down chafing dishes, cans of Sterno, and items to decorate the tables. I've assumed the role of event manager for this party. Even though we have catering captains assigned to each event, I generally look after our repeat customers since I know the hosts personally and I'm often familiar with many of the guests from prior years.

My assistant returns an hour later with the van full of the china and linens we've rented. I put her to work rolling sets of silverware up into napkins while I check with our chef to see if he's made plans for a quick lunch for the staff. I've found that if I don't specifically call a halt, our employees may never stop for a break. With ten hours of work staring us in the face, it's important for us to eat while we can.

Noon is here before we know it. More than half the prep work is done and everything looks to be on schedule for our planned four o'clock departure. On event days we experience a terrific sense of teamwork, with everyone working toward one common goal—to create a great event. Writing out a timeline is a great way to keep everybody on track. Today we arrived at eight o'clock for our prep work, had lunch together at noon, and plan to load the van at 3:00 P.M. for a scheduled departure exactly one hour later. It's a good thing

OUR BARTENDER IS READY TO SERVE.

tonight's event is only a few blocks away, especially with the icy roads.

At two o'clock I confirm with my assistant that we have all the front-of-the-house items we'll need. The silverware has been rolled and china and linens are loaded into the delivery van. Our dock is packed with boxes of glassware, serving items, table décor such as river rocks and flowers, uniforms for our serving staff, and the paperwork we're delivering along with the goodies— multiple copies of tonight's time-line and room layout, plus a copy of the final bill for the host.

In between looking after the prep area, I make intermittent dashes into the office to stay on top of those responsibilities. We make sure to have plenty of staff on hand to prepare for an event but, as an owner, I enjoy being a part of each one as well. After all, I've worked with the clients, created the proposals and organized the menus and the rentals, so there's definitely a sense of ownership going forward. I find no pressing e-mails or voice-mails that need my attention, so back downstairs I go.

Once 3:00 P.M. rolls around a frantic pace takes hold. Nearly every inch of our loading dock is taken up with boxes, equipment and people. Our evening event staff has arrived and helps with the loading while our morning kitchen staff leaves for the day. I refer to this as "The Changing of the Guard," and it's an apt analogy. As the van fills up I sit down with our catering captain to review tonight's game plan. Several weeks ago I met with the event host on location to confirm the table layout and how foot traffic will flow, and we also discussed the night's activities—several speeches to welcome the guests, a review of the rules for the silent auction and then the auction itself, to be followed by dinner and dessert. Tonight's catering captain, an old hat at these events, is raring to go and I'm fully confident she'll make sure this party comes off without a hitch. I remind her I'll be around to answer questions or help out as needed, and then it's time for me to check in with the chef. At four o'clock he gives me a nod, and we climb into our vehicles to head over to the event site. It's time to throw a party!

LESSONS/PROBLEMS

Both the chef and I were concerned about how today's bad weather would affect our event this evening. There were some anxious moments when several of our vendors had difficulty delivering their goods, but everything showed up in plenty of time to be loaded onto our van. Poor weather might reduce the number of guests in attendance, so I called a local homeless shelter later in the day to make sure they'll be open tomorrow for donations, should we have an abundance of food remaining.

MY MARTHA STEWART MINUTE AS I SWITCH OUT THE CHRISTMAS DÉCOR FOR SPRING FLOWERS.

Day 19 | JANUARY 20

PREDICTIONS

- *Review last night's event*
- *Clean up, do the dishes, and return the rented items*

DIARY

Today we're back at the shop early after last night's splendid event. Two of our kitchen staff members are busy sorting through equipment, washing and drying it and then storing it away for the next time we need it. Jeff loads my vehicle with the rented linens and I head off to return them.

When I get back, Jeff and I spend a few minutes discussing last night's event with our kitchen staff. We try to do this after every major catering job. Our front-of-the-house manager had noted in his captain's log that our staff members were helpful and showed up on time, while the bartender was on top of rules and regulations, carding anyone who looked underage and cutting off the only gentleman who seemed to be enjoying the free beer a bit too much. Jeff has little to add regarding the buffet and management in the kitchen, since things went smoothly and everyone played their parts well.

It seems that most of what we do involves cleaning and organizing. After every event it takes a great deal of effort to wash, dry and store everything we used so it's ready for the next party. Each member of our kitchen staff has specific responsibilities in that regard. We carefully examine glassware for cracks, chips, lipstick marks and assorted other stains. Tablecloths frequently come back with wine and food stains, and they need to be properly treated to guarantee many more uses going forward.

One of my responsibilities involves table décor. Oftentimes our candleholders are covered in wax, usually because staffers put warm candles away after an event. Sometimes I have to stand at the dishwashing machine, pouring hot water into each votive and scraping out the wax. If wax has been spilled onto the linens, they must be pre-treated and washed immediately to properly remove it. I also count out the décor items and decide if they need to be replenished. On our buffet tables we have silk flowers, vases, votive candles and river rocks. It may seem strange, but I've noticed over the years that guests will occasionally take home some of these items. If that's the case, I need to replace them before our next event. I'll also arrange our décor items by season to ensure that the kitchen staff assembles the correct ones for each event. Having spring flowers on a Christmas buffet table looks silly, and guests will notice the tiniest of details. Today it appears we've held onto most or all of our table decorations.

EVERYTHING RETURNS TO THE SHOP CAREFULLY STACKED.

Our kitchen manager mentions we're missing a few glasses and plates, due to breakage by guests. One clause in our standard catering contract states that the host will pay for all broken or damaged items. That's why we keep a credit card number on file. If items get damaged, I'll charge them the replacement cost and send an invoice to the host along with a copy of the credit card receipt. That way there aren't any surprises when the charge appears on their monthly statement.

By 2:00 P.M. we've made our way through most of the equipment we used last night, so everyone gets sent home. Jeff figures our school lunch program will resume Monday, so we stay in the kitchen another hour to guarantee we'll start off on the right foot next week. Experience has taught us that anything we do prior to an event puts us well ahead of the game. By three o'clock we've defrosted some chicken and started them marinating, sliced and diced vegetables for the steamed side dish, and baked cookies for dessert.

LESSONS/PROBLEMS

It's important to keep track of return policies when renting items from a vendor. Some rental companies require that different colored linens be kept in separate bags, while others don't seem to care. Some suppliers may ask you to wash and sanitize their dishes and place settings, while others simply want them rinsed. Details are important, or else you might end up paying additional cleaning charges.

TERRILYNN STEPS IN FOR SOME DISH DUTY.

Day 20 | *JANUARY 22*

PREDICTIONS

- *It's a slow day in a slow season*
- *Time for more cleaning and organizing*

DIARY

This week starts out more typical of January than what we've experienced so far this month. In the food service industry, the first quarter is historically the slowest time of the year. When running across fellow caterers, everyone always complains about the slow season and the overall lack of events. Some theorize that people are too busy paying off holiday bills to worry about spending more money on parties. It's also the end of the fiscal year for many companies, and that can put a damper on spending as well.

Since we don't have anything planned this week except for a couple of meetings, we'll focus our efforts on more cleaning and organizing. I'm sure it seems we're always doing that, and that's because we are! With a service-oriented business like catering you're using your tools on a daily basis, and things need to be cleaned and reorganized just as often. If you don't keep up, you may find yourself in the middle of a project and suddenly be lost without a clean pair of serving tongs.

We still have our contract gigs to fulfill, such as the school lunch program and the upcoming literary arts event, so our kitchen continues to hum with food prep while others among us shine and wrap our stainless steel items in anticipation of future events. In the office, the chef and I talk about possible revisions in our marketing strategy. Once a month I meet with our department heads to discuss a variety of topics. This will range from suggested changes in the school lunch program to kudos from clients, and also which trade shows and events are coming to town. As our company's marketing manager, I'm responsible for putting our company's best face forward. This includes updating details on our corporate Web site, making changes to our menu, updating photos and graphics, and designing direct-mail campaigns aimed at both clients and prospects.

This morning our chef suggests we crank up a new marketing effort designed for local schools. Our lunch project is in its second year and going strong, so the model has been proved and we're ready to build up our customer base. My assistant and I put together a list of schools that want to know more, and add some additional likely candidates. Before launching two years ago we did a mass mailing to every private school in the area, letting them know we were starting this kind of program, so we've worked to maintain communications with these schools with twice-yearly marketing campaigns—one early in the year and a second in the fall, as soon as school has begun.

This time around I'll send out postcards as reminders. We've had several newspaper pieces written about our project—free publicity is great for business—so I'll make sure to reference those articles in the mailing, along with photos and testimonials from our current participants. I always make sure our marketing materials are professionally designed. Large photos and quotes from satisfied customers seem to have the greatest impact. We always offer to host an open house for parents, faculty and students for any school that shows serious interest in hiring us to supply their school lunches. While a great picture tells the story in place of a thousand words, providing free samples of the food you make is worth perhaps a million.

We'll schedule any meetings with prospective clients before the school year ends, ensuring our presence at the top of their list of important items to discuss when their respective school boards meet over the summer. We're also redesigning our Web site to include a page devoted exclusively to the lunch program. This is beneficial in a number of ways; it allows potential clients to review our program information, peruse our menus, and learn about seasonal menu items and manufacturer promotions. Because we operate as a sustainable business, we work hard to keep our paper waste down and consequently use a small postcard to guide interested parties onto our Web site for additional information. How did we ever live without the Internet?

Once our marketing meeting is over, the chef heads downstairs to finalize details for today's lunch menu and instruct the staff on the rest of the day's tasks. I begin laying out the graphics for our lunch program postcard, planning to have it printed in mid-February and mailed by the end of that month.

LESSONS/PROBLEMS

I keep an updated marketing schedule handy to stay in touch with customers and potential clients. While most companies tend to bombard you with marketing materials throughout the year, we stick to our sustainable, earth-friendly practices by keeping our print materials to a minimum. In order to eliminate additional waste, anyone on our mailing list can choose removal via e-mail. You can't define your company as a sustainable enterprise and then contribute to enormous amounts of paper waste, or else your customers will wonder what other principles you've compromised.

PREDICTIONS

- Proceed with designing the lunch program postcard
- Begin revising our 2007 menu

DIARY

I awake this morning with a major chest cold and elect to work from home rather than risk infecting the rest of our staff. There's nothing worse than being in the food industry and passing a cold from one employee to another. No one wants to eat food prepared by a kitchen team that's coughing and sneezing. This morning I'll continue to work on the postcard for our school lunch program. I try to come up with two or three designs, after which I'll ask our chef and our lunch program manager to help decide the one that might work best. I toil away until around 11:00 A.M., when I decide to focus for a while on revising our menu. Every December we begin to review menu choices for the upcoming year, taking into account our most popular items, what seems to move the least, and any expected price changes from our suppliers. There have been quite a few issues over the past six months regarding the availability of certain types of produce, so we'll need to factor that into the 2007 menu. I'm also a fan of change, so I like to adjust our layout every so often. I believe change helps keep things interesting, and I'm hopeful our clients will agree.

Our previous menu was formatted to 5" x 7" paper so it

would fit into a specially designed envelope. We've long since run out of them, so I'm seriously contemplating a move to letter-size paper. This new format may not stand out as well as the old one, but it will probably save us money since we won't need to buy those special envelopes.

Almost immediately I identify several items we'll be pulling from our standing menu. In years past we'd had requests for tea sandwiches—oddly enough, that included a casino night with a Harley Davidson theme—but since officially adding them to the menu not one order has been placed. Consequently, they're gone. Another item I was convinced would be popular due to client requests were Thai peanut tofu skewers. No dice, so goodbye tofu!

I'm also adding back some things we'd dropped from our 2006 menu. These were selections requested often enough to warrant reappearance, including our Mediterranean platter, which consists of homemade hummus, pita triangles, and an assortment of vegetables and feta cheese. Our handmade spanikopita also made it back into the menu. It's a mélange of sautéed onions and garlic mixed with spinach and feta and baked in a light phyllo pastry triangle. We'll also bring back our New York cheesecake with seasonal berry sauce. Our barbeque and picnic menus have proven quite popular, so the chef has been busy creating additional dishes to post there. We've also found that most folks like all-inclusive menus rather than building up meals item by item, so we've decided to replace our a la carte menu with one that contains a number of all-in-one buffets.

STUCK AT HOME BUT STILL FOCUSED ON WORK.

This year we're introducing a children's menu. Clients often have difficulty gauging how much food a child will eat, and also what they're willing to eat, so this should help ease their pain. The research we've done in regard to our school lunch program has prepared us well in deciding what to offer our young guests at weddings and other events. Among our selections will be such kid-friendly choices as chicken fingers and spaghetti with meatballs. At one recent wedding we offered PB&J sandwiches cut into various shapes like stars and triangles. Those were an instant hit, and many of the parents in attendance were pleased they didn't have to force feed their children pesto-encrusted salmon or shiitake mushroom risotto.

Due to the bad weather some parts of our country experienced recently, a great many produce items have increased dramatically in price, including avocados and broccoli. In 2006 there was a severe shortage of spinach, something we use frequently in many of our recipes, due to the risk of E. coli bacteria infection. Naturally these are unforeseeable circumstances and require a certain amount of last-minute accommodation. Since we're already aware of the cost increases for avocados and broccoli, our menu pricing will be adjusted accordingly. It's not something we enjoy doing, but we need to keep our profit margins at a certain level in order to stay in business. We also include a disclaimer on our menu that states pricing is subject to change without notice.

Late in the day I've mocked up a preliminary draft of our 2007 menu that includes the proposed changes mentioned above. My next step is to meet again with our chef and review anything else that might prompt pricing changes or additional items worth deleting. At this rate I expect to finalize the new menu by the end of the week.

LESSONS/PROBLEMS

We're extra-careful to stay on top of changes in price and availability for our menu items. Doing so not only saves money but also keeps our clients from being disappointed. I always double-check costs with my kitchen staff as well, since they may have more up-to-date information on such staples as rice or flour.

PREDICTIONS

- *Continue my revisions on our 2007 menu*
- *Review marketing and implementation plans, plus our Web site content*

DIARY

Despite the fact I'm still pretty sick, I force myself into the office this morning for a couple of hours. I bring with me a preliminary layout for our new menu as well as several post-card ideas, and I'd like some feedback before I move forward with printing any of them. At 10:00 A.M., once our school lunch responsibilities are over, I meet with our chef and kitchen manager to look over the new menu layout. Both give their thumbs-up for the overall look, although I suffer an attack of second thoughts and mark up my copy with plenty of red ink. Suddenly this margin looks too big, that font looks too small, and maybe this piece would look better over here. I'm always more critical of my work than anyone else.

I'm pleased that few major changes are called for. The chef decides he'd like to have BBQ/picnic items on one menu and children's items on a separate menu, mostly for the opportunity to feature them individually on the Web site, since each appeals to a different clientele. With the BBQ/picnic menu, we can wait a bit to finalize what's on it in order to promote seasonal products. By eleven o'clock we're finished with this

PAM GRABS HER GLOVES BEFORE
HEADING OUT TO THE SCHOOL.

exercise and both my colleagues head back to the kitchen
to continue their regular duties. After retrieving several telephone messages from my desk, I head home to finish my
day's work and nurse my lingering cold.

I'm home by noon to begin tweaking what is quickly turning into our 2007 menu package. I've also received a voice-
mail message from someone seeking a facility for his food
product line. Over the years we've had quite a few people,
friends as well as strangers, ask to rent our kitchen for their
own endeavors. We have 2200 square feet that includes the
kitchen, a walk-in refrigerator, a large storage room, office
space, and a small meeting room. It's an ideal location for
anyone who wants to pursue his or her food service dream.
However, our landlord is adamantly against sub-leasing, and

rightfully so. When you allow your tenant to sub-lease space to others, you're always worried that the sub-lessee will use it in non-acceptable ways or fail to have the proper licensing in place. In addition to that, a kitchen environment has specific health codes and I'm not willing to risk our license because a sub-lessee decides to leave dirty dishes lying around or fails to label foodstuffs correctly.

More out of curiosity than anything else, I decide to return the man's phone call. He explains that a small manufacturing firm in town employs him. They're looking for a kitchen and a staff that can produce his company's recipes at the ingredients level and then package everything for further production and distribution. He has a whole horde of questions for me. Has the USDA licensed us? Has the Oregon Tilth, a local organic certification group, inspected our facility? How large is our staff? How many cubic feet of spare refrigeration capacity do we have? I try to answer his questions as best I can—without giving too much away —and I ask him to send me written information about his operation. If the chef and I have any further interest, I'll call him back and arrange a tour of our facility. He appears satisfied with my responses and we agree to discuss this again next week.

Once I'm off the phone I take a moment to review any proposals that might need revising. We have quite a few preliminary proposals in a folder labeled "In Process," including one for an upcoming literary arts event plus numerous weddings and summer get-togethers. Nothing seems terribly pressing at the moment, so I turn my attention back to finalizing our new menus. Two hours later, after I've tweaked and adjusted them as much as I can stand, I turn my attention to our corporate Web site. Not only do the menus need to be updated online, but I also plan to switch out photos, change the content on our home page, and add new testimonials from our clients. Since over the next thirty days we're turning our focus to school lunches, I decide to include photos and details on that program on our home page. With that mailing coming up soon, I want to have new information posted online for people to see when they visit our Web site.

By the time four o'clock rolls around I'm ready to call it a day and head back to bed. Just as I'm shutting down my computer, a call comes into the office. By having our business calls forwarded to my home office, it's easier to deal with them when they occur rather than making a whole bunch of callbacks the next day.

"Hi there," says the man on the phone. "My name is George, and I'm calling from Citysearch.com, where you have been chosen Portland's best caterer for 2007. Our voting period just ended and I wanted to call personally to congratulate you!"

"Why, thank you," I reply.

"I see you've won for the second year in a row," he continues, "even though you've only been in business for four years. Wow, that's impressive!"

"Yes it is," I respond, smiling to myself. It's a nice way to end the workday.

LESSONS/PROBLEMS

Today we had one more request to "borrow" our kitchen facilities. Caterers get asked this all the time, especially if they have a great location. We always make sure to review all possible requirements when it comes to sub-leasing, both with our landlord and with the appropriate local, state or federal entities. We also ask ourselves if the money we stand to earn would compensate adequately for the worries we might encounter over someone else's operation.

WORKING ON THE WEBSITE WHILE STILL RECOVERING AT HOME.

Day 23 | JANUARY 25

PREDICTIONS

- *Finalize marketing projects, our menu, and other materials*
- *Confirm staff interviews for Friday.*

DIARY

Still recuperating from my cold, it's yet another day best worked from home. We have to be very careful, particularly with the lunch program. One person's illness can infect our lunch prep staff, which may in turn pass along the cold to the whole school. That would be ugly!

This morning I'm wrapping up the postcards we'll use to promote the school lunch program. Jeff and I have already decided on a design and a layout, so today I'll arrange to have them printed. I'm guessing we'll need 100 for our first mailing. I also take an hour to finalize the content on our Web site. We'd already posted the new menu and I've changed our home page to highlight our school lunches. Recently we've received quite a few proposal requests via the "Contact Us" link on our site. One of those events is a large company's ribbon-cutting ceremony in Vancouver, Washington, a city to the north of Portland and right across the river. I place a call to the contact person to find out more, and she tells me they're expecting 75–100 guests for brunch at the end of February. The company is relocating their corporate headquarters from San Francisco, so she wants it to be a really nice event. She has a $3000 budget to cover a full-service wait staff with tables and chairs, linens, china and silverware, and a full buffet that will include both breakfast and lunch items. We agree to meet the following week, and I begin a preliminary proposal for her event.

Even though we have a new client worksheet for reference, I have most of the questions memorized now that we're four years into the business. Important things to know include whether there are any food allergies or restrictions (yes, a vegan option has been requested), if beverage service should be included (yes, they want coffee and tea), and whether there is a strict timeline of events to follow (no, speeches will be given while the food is being served). Receiving a preliminary proposal is a great way for a client to begin preparations for an event. The paperwork allows them to review menu options in addition to pricing. It includes a list of suggested rental items as well. We've found that many of our clients appreciate having a preliminary proposal to produce at board meetings or staff meetings so their co-workers or supervisors will understand what's going on.

Once I've created a proposal for this event and e-mailed it to her, I focus on confirming tomorrow's appointments. Since placing an ad online for additional serving staff, we've received quite a few resumes via e-mail. However, there are generally only a few resumes that truly fit the criteria we require. I've narrowed the field to eight possible candidates, four of whom are set to meet with me tomorrow. I prefer to confirm these interviews both by telephone and e-mail. All too often I've relied on e-mail alone, only to find that people aren't checking their inboxes on a regular enough basis. This has unfortunately resulted in a few missed connections, so a backup phone call or voice message is always a good idea.

This time of year is traditionally a slow one for caterers, so I often use some online resources to help bring in new business. There are a number of Web sites where people post their impending events. This information is then submitted to local purveyors to generate multiple bids. In our earliest days, these Web sites served as our primary sources for upcoming events. They often charge a small fee to list you as a supplier, and some even ask for a percentage of the revenue if the lead turns into a client, but in general it's a great option for anyone just starting out in the business. These leads are automatically distributed via e-mail or fax, so it's easy to review event requests and respond as needed. This time of year almost everything is a wedding lead, so I take an hour to respond to as many as I can. While many of them are not in our service area—such as several for Bellingham, Washington, a city two hours north of Seattle and at least five hours from us—I find a few intriguing possibilities and respond accordingly.

LESSONS/PROBLEMS

This entire week has been slow, which is hardly unusual for this time of the year. I'm a big fan of the standard restaurant edict, "If there's time to lean, there's time to clean," although I tend to take it more figuratively than literally. This is my time to review our marketing materials and our Web presence, "cleaning up" any loose ends and brainstorming new ways to get our name out there. There are lots of ways to dig up leads without cold-calling companies around town, which is not my cup of tea. Those lead-generation Web sites don't cost all that much, and they can pay for themselves with just one job.

PREDICTIONS

- *Hold interviews for new serving staffers*
- *Confirm next week's parties and the staff to work them*

DIARY

Today's top priority is to interview four people for the position of server. Randie is scheduled at 10:00 A.M., Matt at 11:00, June at 1:00 P.M., and Chris at 2:00. Each has prior catering experience and looks to be a great addition to our staff, at least on paper.

Before that, however, I need to confirm some last-minute details on two events scheduled for next week. On Monday evening a law firm is entertaining some out-of-town clients, and Thursday evening is our party for the literary arts group. Monday's event is a reasonably large one, with around 100 guests for cocktails and hors d'oeuvres. The law firm's office is downtown, in the hip area of the Pearl District, and will require a few small cocktail tables as well as linens and china plates. Since we're providing butlered hors d'oeuvres we'll need seven staff members—two to work the back of the house by prepping the hors d'oeuvres and replenishing platters, plus five staff members to mingle through the crowd. It looks to be a pretty basic event for us. Their menu includes baked Brie on sliced baguettes, prawn cocktails, wild-mushroom potstickers, and marinated vegetables. When we provide a passed hors d'oeuvres service and the client requests baked Brie, we provide the cheese pre-portioned on baguette slices. During the summer these are topped with raspberries or a strawberry slice. During the winter and fall we offer apple slices or roasted garlic. Some clients turn down the garlic option for conversational purposes, but the law firm is adamant about having the roasted garlic. After phoning the event host to confirm the details, I send a quick e-mail to my five front-of-the-house staffers to remind them of the event.

Thursday's menu is a bit simpler and will be served buffet style. The crowd of literary arts patrons is quite particular about their food, so we're including four of our most popular hors d'oeuvres items. We've also had a special request for vegetarian items, since the guest speaker is a vegetarian. Nearly three-quarters of our menu items fall into this category, so that won't be a problem. We've selected sage-and-garlic-stuffed mushrooms, a domestic cheese platter served with crackers, marinated vegetables, and our Zen Bananas for dessert. We have a regular staff that works each of these literary events, so I send a quick e-mail to the three staff members to confirm their attendance as well. Then I take twenty minutes to place an online order with our rental company for Monday's event, following up with a phone call to make sure everything went through all right. Now it's time for my first interview.

Randie had e-mailed me earlier in the week to ask about rescheduling her interview, since her babysitter cancelled. I assured her we're a family-friendly establishment, so she arrives with her two beautiful daughters in her arms. Her youngest daughter smiles at me from across the table while we're chatting, pausing briefly to laugh whenever I laugh. Randie has a number of years of serving experience and should be a great addition to our staff. After thirty minutes I thank her for her time and let her know I'll be adding her to our call list.

Matt arrives at 11:00. While he has a solid background in catering and as a server, he doesn't seem all that outgoing or friendly. Whenever I do hiring interviews, I look for a great personality as well as plenty of experience. Many of our clients compliment us on our staff, and I work hard to maintain that level of customer service. I don't see Matt fitting in as we'd like, but I thank him for coming just the same.

After a quick lunch I return to the meeting room to wait for our one o'clock appointment. Interviewees are almost always early or right on time. At 1:15 it's apparent June isn't going to show up, so I return to my office to see if she sent me a message to explain her absence. Half an hour later I run her resume through our paper shredder and prepare for my final interview of the day. Then 2:15 rolls around and it's painfully obvious I've been stood up twice. I realize the position we're offering is part-time and on-call, but I'm still surprised by the number of people who set up interviews yet never show up or even bother to call with an explanation.

LESSONS/PROBLEMS

There were two no-shows today out of four scheduled hiring interviews. If people miss their interviews and don't reschedule, I generally need to repost our online ad in order to dig up additional candidates. It's frustrating, but that's what happens when running your own business.

JEFF MULTITASKS AT THE STOVE.

Day 25 | **JANUARY 29**

PREDICTIONS

- *Prepare for tonight's event*
- *Confirm tomorrow's meeting*

DIARY

Today we're catering an event for 100 guests, and the chef and I arrive early to get things started in the kitchen. I've received quite a few voice-mail messages over the weekend, but the one that concerns me most is from one of our servers. She is suffering from a chest cold. When I return her call she sounds miserable, and it's obvious she won't be able to work this evening. With only one staff member ill I'm able to fill her spot with someone from our kitchen staff, so I tell her not to sweat it and to take care of herself.

I call down and let Jeff know I'll need an extra set of hands to pass the hors d'oeuvres this evening, and he agrees it won't be a problem. Many of our kitchen staffers double as servers to pick up extra cash. He explains our lunch person can do the job, so long as she manages a few hours rest before the event begins. We don't allow our staff to work more than an eight hour shift, because then exhaustion sets in and good service goes downhill. I take a few moments to confirm a meeting for tomorrow with the gentleman who inquired about using our kitchen for manufacturing. For some reason, every time I talk to him on the phone he sounds rather slick, but we've agreed nonetheless to meet with him tomorrow for a tour of our location. He's not immediately available when I call, so I leave him a voice message.

By 11:00 the kitchen is ahead of the game. The school lunch for the day has been packed and is on its way to be deliv-- ered. Most of the prep work is finished for tonight's event, so the kitchen staff begins to garnish the platters. After lunch our final push begins. By two o'clock the kitchen staff starts to pull together the equipment and the food we'll need to- night. The item we seem to forget more than any other is the platter garnish, about which our chef is especially fussy. He employs organic herbs, like rosemary and dill, to dress up his platters, and there's nothing more frustrating than arriv- ing at an event without the garnishes. Well, we've forgotten the dips a few times, too.

PRAWN COCKTAILS AND A MARINATED VEGETABLE PLATTER.

By 4:00 P.M. we're ready to roll out the door for the five o'clock event, scheduled for a downtown law firm. After completing the journey, our staff unloads everything for the trip to the building's 27th floor. Since we don't care to make multiple trips down to the van, we've brought along a number of carts to help ease the move. At 4:30 our bartender crew has arrived as well, and everything starts right on time. With the onset of the cocktail hour, people start to filter in. Based on the demographics, this party seems meant to serve as a meet-and-greet for partners and spouses as well as a welcome for out-of-town visitors. Everyone acts in a friendly manner, and our staff is clearly on top of their duties. I mingle with the crowd while keeping an eye on the servers who rotate through the room while carrying our goodies on their trays.

I've found catering to be quite an interesting business. At some events we're treated like culinary gods, with guests and clients asking food-related questions and complimenting us on everything from our smiles to our crispy baguette slices. But at other times, such as tonight, we're looked upon as hired help, with guests asking us to fetch them more wine or hold doors open for arriving guests. You can always tell the people who have worked in food service, however, because they always treat you with the utmost respect.

LESSONS/PROBLEMS

In advance of tonight's event I made sure to obtain as many specific details of the party location as possible. That's especially important if the event is being held in a high-traffic area. I always ask our clients for advice regarding the best place to park, whether a security office needs to be notified of our arrival, and how the entrances are situated. This can save a lot of grief once you show up. In our early days, all too often we'd arrive without carts or parking instructions, making things ten times more difficult on ourselves for setup or breakdown. Buildings may be equipped with dedicated service entrances and reserved parking for deliveries—oftentimes more convenient than patron parking—so it's usually beneficial to ask as many questions as possible.

PREDICTIONS

- *Cleanup and organization*
- *Review last night's event*
- *Meet with the manufacturer's rep*
- *Continue dealing with staffing needs*

DIARY

Last night's event went very well. Even though we were one person short for the front of the house, we dispatched a kitchen worker several times throughout the evening to carry food through the crowd. Everyone seemed pleased with the service and the menu selections, and the host expressed her appreciation to us once the event was over.

Just the same, by the time we got home last night it had turned out to be another fourteen-hour day for us. Owning a catering business is much less glamorous than it may seem on the Food Network. Mario and Emeril are joyful every time you tune into their programs, but that's because they're celebrity chefs. Behind the scenes they have an army of workers who prep their food and clean up after them. Our favorite celebrity chef is Anthony Bourdain, who isn't afraid to discuss how these long hours can lead to unfortunate personal situations. Cooking isn't necessarily glamorous, and running a catering service can lack excitement. There are days when you work only a few hours, and there are days when you don't remember what your dog looks like. You have to be prepared to put in some serious effort if you want to make it big. It's a long road, but there are some great rewards along the way.

We arrive at the kitchen around ten o'clock, a bit later than usual. Our kitchen staff has already started on the school's lunch menu. Jeff settles into his office, checking e-mails and making phone calls to confirm upcoming food deliveries. It's also a chance to relax from yesterday's mass hysteria. This turns into one of those "it's good to be the boss" moments. Jeff and I take some time to discuss last night's event and review areas where changes might be needed. Both of us feel the evening was an overall success, with only a couple of minor problems. The client told us to expect 100 guests, but close to 150 showed up. That could be a recipe for disaster, but we try to plan for such eventualities and managed to handle the additional crowd because we brought along extra servings of marinated vegetables and baked Brie. The only difficulty with the additional guest count was running out of wine glasses. Midway through the event we started serving wine in the extra pilsner glasses we carry, which the host didn't seem to mind. Jeff's primary concern was staff members in the rear prep area who helped themselves to items once they came back to the kitchen from the serving floor. We frown upon such things, as I believe it reflects negatively on our company and the professionalism of our staff. If I'm hosting an event for which I paid $3000 for catering services, I'd be upset to find workers eating food items before the party was over. The primary culprit was a new staff member who hadn't done much work for us, and we managed to nip the situation in the bud before it became a widespread problem. While you're a business owner, sometimes you end up taking on a parenting role as well.

At noon we meet Paul, a gentleman from a company in search of manufacturing space. They're interested in subleasing a kitchen and staff to cook high-end organic products and then transport them to a separate location for packaging and labeling. He comes equipped with a list of additional licensing requirements we'd have to satisfy in order to produce such items. After only a few minutes touring our facility he seems dismayed at our location, which is just as well since the volume of equipment we'd need to purchase in order to perform the necessary processing tasks equally dismays Jeff and me. We sit down and chat a bit more about his expectations but ultimately agree our location and space would not be a good fit for what he requires.

By two o'clock I'm back in my office, focused on the insufficient number of skilled workers we have on our call list. Because my interviews last week went so poorly, I elect to repost an online request to search of additional staff members. I'm holding five resumes from the previous round that seem interesting, so I send out e-mails to ask whether they are still interested in an interview. By the time I'm ready to leave for the day, I have two interviews set up for next week. We'll see if anyone works out, or shows up!

LESSONS/PROBLEMS

Two issues needed addressing from last night's event—running out of wine glasses, and staff members who fed themselves from platters behind closed doors. Both situations required immediate attention. We often keep a stack of disposable cups in our delivery van, just in case we have an unexpected increase in guests. While there is clear language in our contract that we're not responsible for running out of food or rental items if additional guests show up, we still try to remain professional at all times and accommodate them as best we can. As for the staff members who munched on leftover food before the event ended, they needed only a quick talk to put a stop to their sticky fingers.

PREDICTIONS

- *Close the month by reviewing parties and sales*
- *Prepare for the literary event*

DIARY

Upon arriving at the office I'm pleased to discover my inbox filled with e-mails in response to our help-wanted posting. Once I wade through my voice-mail messages I'll start checking over the resumes that were submitted. Quite a few calls have come in regarding parties for this summer. Two more couples planning weddings also wish to meet with us, and there's an inquiry by a local veterinary hospital planning an open house in March. That's the call I return first, reaching Paula to answer her questions about our catering options. For their location in southeast Portland they're seeking someone to provide an all-organic menu and adhere to some dietary restrictions, including nut allergies and a call for vegan items. Our work with the school lunch program has boosted our ability to accommodate such requests. A number of students in the program either suffer from food allergies or require vegetarian and vegan selections, and working with them has improved our ability to adapt the rest of our menu accordingly. Paula selects a number of hors d'oeuvres including baked Brie on sliced baguettes, spinach-and-feta phyllo cups, ginger beef skewers, and chocolate-dipped strawberries, which will cost a bit extra to track down

JEFF AND A BIT OF THE PREP LIST. OUR WORK IS NEVER DONE.

off-season. She'll add to those items a seasonal crudités platter and a marinated vegetable platter to cover all her bases. I promise to e-mail her a proposal within the hour, and I'll phone tomorrow as a follow-up.

I place calls to both couples that phoned in, leaving voice-mail messages as I imagine they're at work. Our office hours generally run weekdays from 9:00 A.M. to 6:00 P.M., which helps us to accommodate as many working people as possible. Then I find time to sit down with our chef to review our sales and event statistics from the month that ends today. I try to stay on top of our sales on a weekly as well as monthly basis. Doing so not only gives us a better idea of where we stand regarding sales goals, but it also allows us to keep track of our numbers for end-of-the-year tax purposes. This month is comparable to most other Januarys we've experienced—much slower than our busiest months but still acceptable. We've catered a total of seven events this month, allowing us to break even, which is pretty much all you can expect during your first few years in business. Having added a number of new clients to our roster, I consider it a successful month overall. Jeff reports that supplies are running low in the kitchen, just as we'd planned, so a large food order will be necessary within the week to bring our inventory back to appropriate levels. The school lunch program is going smoothly, with the children seeming to adapt well to the five-day hot lunch plan, and feedback from parents has been positive. There are a few lunch menu items we'll ditch for next month, but the changes we implemented at the beginning of the semester are proving worthwhile.

Our next party is tomorrow evening—another literary arts event. When we were awarded the contract last summer, I was ecstatic to find out that the deal came with a bunch of goodies, including tickets to each speaker's event and autographed copies of their books. When catering for Stephen King last the fall, I was thrilled to hear him speak and take home his latest novel. Tomorrow's event hosts a pair of editors who created the "Best American" literary series. We've been asked to supply a mostly vegetarian menu, since both speakers adhere to that diet. I send over a quick e-mail to the event director to confirm our menu selection and event times, and then I'm ready to start on my pile of resumes.

But first I receive a call from a local school that's seeking a donation for a silent auction they're holding in April. We pride ourselves on donating to the greater Portland area, which includes items for silent auctions and fundraisers as well as foodstuffs to local homeless shelters. People enjoy patronizing businesses that benefit their community, and it's a great opportunity for Jeff and me to support our favorite social causes. I copy down the woman's contact information and tell her we'll be happy to donate something. It only takes a few minutes for me to e-mail her one of our standard donation packets, complete with a menu, a color brochure, and a gift certificate.

LESSONS/PROBLEMS

We received a phone call today for a donation to a local fundraiser. We feel it's important to support our local community in this manner. It's just as important to keep track of donations, since they're tax deductible. In 2006 we over-extended ourselves in this regard, so I'm trying to be more cautious this year. We stick to a selection of hors d'oeuvres for most donations. Naturally we'd love to give away an entire event, but that would not be a business-savvy decision no matter what kind of exposure it brought us.

PREDICTIONS

- Cater the literary arts event
- Schedule interviews to hire additional staffers

DIARY

Today we're prepping for this evening's literary arts event. It's been a regular gig for us for quite a while, so the anxiety level is considerably lessened. Since the location, the time and the guest count remains the same from one party to the next—with a rotating menu the only option—we can pretty much put our crew on autopilot. I'm at the office by 9:00 A.M., and most of our kitchen staff is in the midst of school lunch prep. Others have begun the initial organization for the literary arts event. Tonight we're serving a marinated vegetable platter, a domestic cheese platter with crackers, sage-and-garlic-stuffed mushrooms, and a platter of assorted cookies. As usual we expect to serve from 200–250 guests.

Once I see everything in the kitchen is under control, I head up to my office for the day. It's payroll time once again, so I spend the first hour reviewing everyone's time cards and calling our payroll provider with the numbers. Just as our events change from one week to the next, so does our payroll. When we first opened our doors, I planned to handle all the payroll duties myself. After all, I had no problem keeping my household accounts under control. But once I received all the paperwork from the state regarding a myriad of regulations—each one seemingly more confusing than the next—it made sense to let the experts handle everything. As a result our unemployment insurance, worker's compensation insurance and tax payments are submitted on time, and I don't have to worry about forgetting to send something in. One important rule in business is to assign people to the tasks for which they're best suited. My strong suit is definitely not payroll. After a quick phone call to our provider I stash the timecards in each employee's file and continue with my office duties.

My inbox is starting to fill up with e-mailed resumes for the server positions we've advertised and I spend an hour reviewing them, printing out the ones that show the greatest promise. Just the same, we continue to receive responses from people who lack server and catering experience. One woman has a brilliant background in science, including a degree in geology, but her resume mentions no work in a restaurant let alone with a caterer. Another woman recently graduated from a top-notch culinary school in New York and is seeking a full-time position. Neither is the right candidate for us, with one missing vital know-how and the other expecting a forty-hour workweek, which we're not offering. After wading through thirty responses I end up with seven reasonably acceptable resumes. I respond via e-mail and let everyone know we're scheduling interviews for next week. I'm hopeful this round of interviews will yield at least a couple of superior candidates.

WHEN GUESTS ATTACK!

Before I know it, it's lunchtime. In between bites, Jeff and I talk over what remains to be done in preparation for tonight's event. Food prep appears to be almost complete, and soon the kitchen staff will start building initial platters. Our planned departure time is 6:00 P.M., and the event starts at 8:30. The party usually lasts only an hour or so, and that time always goes by quickly.

After lunch is finished I start working on my front-of-the-house task—organizing the table décor. Since it's nearly spring and certainly no longer part of the holiday season, it's time to change out our decorations. I recently bought some beautiful silk flowers for the tables as well as some spare petals for placement in the candle hurricanes that oc-cupy the center of the buffet tables. Some caterers decorate with food, scattering the tabletop with rolls and small loaves

WE COMPOST AND RECYCLE AT EVERY EVENT.

of bread, while others spend a considerable amount on live floral decorations. We prefer to take a middle ground, keeping the table clean and accessible while incorporating tasteful décor. For fall events we include silk leaves, some with a hint of glitter, which really spices up the tables. In the spring our preference runs to silk flowers and river rocks. At the trade shows we cater we'll also feature fruits and vegetables, which highlights the fresh, organic nature of our business. We're given kudos on our simple and elegant table décor as often as we're complimented on our food and staff.

While the kitchen staff is busy assembling the equipment we'll need this evening, I park myself in our meeting room and focus on updating the décor. Once I've gathered up our hurricane lamps, menus and flowers, I drag out the linens we'll need for the buffet and beverage tables. I also collect the mandarin shirts our staff members wear at every event. These are expensive items so I keep them dry-cleaned. A caterer's servers are the first people noticed at any event, and it's vital that our staff looks pressed and professional at all times.

The event proceeds marvelously, as usual. The marketing director stops by to review the room before things get started, and I join her at the lecture while our staff prepares for the reception. After the speakers have had their say, the executive director escorts the guests to the buffet. We've anticipated their needs by having glasses of wine and bottles of water standing by, as well as several plates of food assembled prior to the mad rush of guests. Even though this event is a short one, the crowd seems to come in like a cloud of locusts, devouring everything in the room. I always make sure we reserve food for our honored guests, who tend to arrive late at the reception because they're usually interacting with members of the audience. We also do this at all our wedding receptions, for obvious reasons. You never want the guest of honor to miss out on the food!

This event proves a bit difficult for me to attend, since I'm well along in my pregnancy. I'm used to operating as a very hands-on owner, taking an active role by moving tables and chairs, picking up plates and glasses as they're set down in various locations, and helping out our servers wherever necessary. Jeff is often forced to pull me aside and remind me to take it easy. We always have enough staff members on hand but, as a proprietor, I take great pride in every party we ca-

SOMEHOW, JEFF ALWAYS MANAGES TO GET A FEW KISSES IN.

ter. I'm usually dressed in my finery in order to meet with the host and mingle with the guests, but I always seem to manage some work. After four years of owning this business, it's in my blood. It's not just a job—it's a party each time, and I like being part of the action. I enjoy a great sense of pride with every event, and I can't let a little thing like pregnancy stand in my way.

LESSONS/PROBLEMS

I'm still not all that happy with the response we've received for our open serving positions. Once we interview this current crop of candidates, I may need to call a local placement company and discuss setting up serving placements for a few of our larger upcoming events. As usual, in catering it pays to have an alternative plan—just in case!

PREDICTIONS

- *Ship off box lunches*
- *Meet with an event planner for an upcoming silent auction*
- *Deal with bartending issues*

DIARY

Last night's event went very well, except for one issue with the bartending staff. We supply our own glassware, and apparently some were still lipstick-stained when they were handed to guests. Eww! Since lipstick is made up of all sorts of chemicals, your only two choices for ensuring tip-top cleanliness involves washing glassware at very high temperatures—we own a low-temp dishwasher—or else scrubbing each one of them by hand to remove the makeup. It's apparent we missed a few glasses when sorting through them before the event. That caused a bit of a tiff with the bartenders, who weren't happy with the dirty glasses. It didn't turn into a major problem because we addressed it immediately.

We spend our morning cleaning and putting away our equipment. On the food service side, in addition to our standing school lunch delivery, we also have box lunches going to a party of fifteen out in Lake Oswego, just south of the city. The school lunches are out the door promptly at 11:00, and our delivery guy has already loaded up and left for Lake Oswego. I love it when people order box lunches, since one magically appears on my desk at lunchtime as well.

PAM CLEANS UP THE PREP TABLE.

This afternoon I'm meeting with an event planner currently in the process of arranging a plated dinner for 200 guests at a local natural history museum. This event will honor Earth Day, April 22, and she's eager to start her planning as early as possible. Based on the size and complexity of the event we'll need additional staffing for both the back and the front of the house. Samantha and I sit down at one o'clock to review her menu selections. The entrée is a choice of Burgundy beef tips or wild salmon with cilantro-mango salsa. Side dishes include roasted seasonal vegetables plus garden rice pilaf, as well as tossed field greens for the salad course. For dessert we'll serve New York cheesecake with seasonal berry sauce, each slice topped with a sprig of mint. In addition to these selections she wants a vegan/vegetarian alternative, and we decide on grilled vegetable skewers. We also make a preliminary list of the tables, chairs, linens, china, silverware and glassware we'll need to supply for the occasion. There will be a cash bar, so I provide her with the information on our bartending partners. She promises me she'll have a proper headcount—including food selections—no later than early April. We agree to meet again in March to finalize everything and also perform a walkthrough of the location. No matter how many times we've catered a spot, I always do a walkthrough with our staff prior to the event. That's especially important for large and/or plated events, because it gives our people a chance to review the evening's game plan without having any last-minute surprises sprung on them.

I return to my office after the meeting, while the kitchen staff heads home for the day and Jeff starts prepping for a small party we're catering on Sunday—Super Bowl Sunday! There are a few phone messages for me regarding upcoming events, including a wedding in July, but all I get when returning those calls is voice mail. After starting our catering business we received numerous requests from people we know to cater even the smallest of their social gatherings. We're happy to do them—after all, I'm pleased to show off my husband's culinary skills—and you never know when one of these events will lead to big business. It's better yet when we cater something like a family holiday gathering and actually get to eat the food we've prepared!

At three o'clock I enter the kitchen to assist Jeff with the last bit of kitchen prep for tomorrow's event. We're not bringing much table décor with us, and there aren't large quantities of glassware or plates to assemble, so I'm able to take my time gathering things together. I'm mentally prepared for my responsibilities tomorrow—mushrooms, baguettes and vegetables—as I sit down at our white board and make a list of prep tasks for when we show up at the kitchen in the morning. Anything I can do a day ahead of time helps in the overall picture. Forethought and preparation are keys to a successful business, especially in the food service industry.

LESSONS/PROBLEMS

I've learned that even when utilizing in-house items, problems may arise with equipment, such as missing plates, stained tablecloths, and linens that are slightly mismatched. In the catering business, it's always something. But if you're prepared to handle whatever gets thrown your way, you'll be fine.

SOMETIMES I'M ON KITCHEN DUTY.

Day 30 | **FEBRUARY 4**

PREDICTIONS

- *Cater a Super Bowl party for friends*
- *Review the month's highlights*
- *Make predictions for the upcoming season*

DIARY

We're in our commercial kitchen by 10:00 A.M., having arranged to cater a party for friends this afternoon who are gathering to watch the Super Bowl on TV. Our contribution involves a number of hors d'oeuvres platters, so we're here to prep. This week's events went well, and we have some cleaning and organizing tasks to handle prior to getting started on the food. Only Jeff and I are in the kitchen today.

JEFF SHOWS OFF HIS COOKING SKILLS.

These are nostalgic times for us, since that's the way we started out four years ago. Running a catering business together has been very good for our marriage, although most people cringe in horror when I tell them we work together. Over the last four years we've learned to get along in any situation, under occasionally extreme pressure, and even when we have arguments over who forgot to bring enough sugar packets. We started this business early in our courtship and now we're married and expecting a child, so something must be working!

Today's menu for the Super Bowl party includes Thai peanut chicken skewers, a crudités platter with garden herb dip, mushrooms stuffed with Italian sausage, and baked Brie on sliced baguettes. We decided to go heartier since we recognize our guests will be drinking during the football game, and full-bodied food does a better job of absorbing alcohol. And since it's a personal event, there's definitely a lack of stress while we get things ready.

My kitchen responsibilities are the usual ones—clean and core the mushrooms, create the stuffed mushroom mix, wash the vegetables, slice the baguettes, and toast the bread pieces. Jeff handles most of the knife work, cutting up a number of chicken breasts and slicing the vegetables. Once things are prepped we start laying out platters for the event, storing them in the refrigerator until it's time to depart. The chicken skewers are placed in aluminum containers and kept hot in the oven until we're ready to leave. Even though it's Sunday, I run up to the office and check my voice-mail messages. There are none requiring immediate attention—our insurance agent, someone seeking a full-time chef's position, and a message from a woman planning an event in July—so I return to the kitchen and assist Jeff with gathering up our food platters and equipment.

The past thirty days have been active ones, representing an average catering month. We have a few events booked for February and March and a number already scheduled for summer—two events in May, three in June, two in July, and five in August. It should prove be a very busy summer for us, especially with the baby coming. On our way to the party, Jeff and I discuss these events and also talk about where we'd like to be by the end of the year. It's our goal to double last year's sales, just as we've done for the past four years. We've been blessed with plenty of repeat business and terrific referrals from friends and family ever since opening our business, and we're excited to watch it continue to grow.

When March comes, we'll review the fall school year and try to gauge how many schools we'll be able to add to the program, as well as calculate the maximum number of students we'll be able to serve. We already have serious inquiries from three new schools, so we'll begin meeting with representative of each of them to determine what's possible for everyone involved. We think it's a great program, and we look forward to expanding it in years to come.

Everyone heralds our arrival at the party. After all, we're not supplying your basic chips and dip here. That's usually the case among our circle of friends. We tend to be the highlight of the party, as most of our friends aren't big fans of cooking for themselves. Also, Jeff gets regular phone calls from friends and family who pelt him with cooking questions. Can I cook the chicken at this temperature? What can I do with a fillet of salmon, two cloves of garlic, and a lemon? It's a difficult job running a catering business, especially because of the long hours and the occasional temperamental customer, but it's a place Jeff and I have built together. We *are* Zen Kitchen, and we're immensely proud of our creation.